PRAISE FOR *THE*

"A must-read book for everyone serious about taking their teams further, faster."

—Justin Patton
Award-Winning Author of *Bold New You*

"Mark Kenny is a master storyteller, and he delivers with his terrific new book, *The Hippo Solution*. For organizations and leaders who want to figure out how to work as a team to improve productivity and morale, this book is a must-read. Mark gives the reader practical advice and makes it memorable through his excellent stories. Highly recommended."

—Cathy Fyock
The Business Book Strategist

"Mark Kenny delivers a compelling, practical approach for leaders to develop the synergy and collaboration that is needed to deal with today's pace of change. "

—Bryan Luci
Senior Vice President of a nationally
recognized insurance company

"The tips shared in this book have wonderful gems for both your business and work life and for your personal life as well. It is a must read."

—Captain William "T" Thompson, Esq., CSP
CEO, Strategist, Professional Speaker

"*The Hippo Solution* is exactly what I've been looking for and a must-read for all leaders. If you want to take your results to a whole new level by using an easy-to-understand and powerful formula for reaching any destination, Mark has the answer."

—Dr. Jason Brooks
Leadership Consultant, Author, Speaker

"Some books you read, and others you live. This one you'll read and then watch it happen again and again! Mark doesn't just peel back the curtain and show the challenges of team-building to which all leaders can relate. He reveals the transformational formula that will bring results you can see!"

—Gary Carter
School Administrator

"The workforce continues to evolve, and Mark's perspective and framework offers leaders valuable insights and, more importantly, real-world applications for how to succeed in the new work world."

—Cara Silletto, MBA, CSP
President & Chief Retention Officer at Magnet Culture

"I work with organizations and leaders at all levels across the globe, and any time I get an inkling of territorial thinking or misalignment in general, *The Hippo Solution* is the first book I recommend they read!"

—Stacy Henry
Professional Certified Coach and Author

"Have you ever worked in a company with incredibly talented people, adequately funded resources, even leadership's blessing and witnessed major projects and initiatives fail? In my years in corporate America, I have seen this occur on more than one occasion. We scratch our heads and ask, "What the heck happened?" In his timely book, Mark Kenny explains how those territorial and stubborn Hippos got in the way. In this masterfully written book, Kenny details the formula to subdue the beasts and, importantly, build a highly functioning team and organization. This book is now a vital addition to my consultant's tool kit."

—Sara L. Potecha
Best Selling Author, Speaker, Executive Coach, and Consultant

The Hippo Solution

*Eliminate Territorial Thinking and
Unleash the Power of Teams*

MARK KENNY

**IGNITE
P R E S S**
Fresno, CA

Published in the United States by
Ignite Press
5070 N 6th St. #189
Fresno, CA 93710
www.IgnitePress.us

ISBN: 978-1-953655-68-4 (Amazon Print)
ISBN: 978-1-953655-69-1 (IngramSpark) PAPERBACK
ISBN: 978-1-953655-70-7 (Ebook)

For bulk purchase and for booking, contact:

info@hipposolutions.com

Library of Congress Control Number: 2021903663

Cover design by Bien Swinton
Edited by Samantha Maxwell
Interior design by Jetlaunch Layout Services

This book is dedicated to my father, Larry Kenny.
Thanks for being a great Dad.
I miss you, and I'm grateful for the years we had together.

ACKNOWLEDGMENTS

This book, like most books, has been a labor of love and involved a community of people that I would like to thank.

First, I'd like to thank Monica, my dear wife, for putting up with my dreams and efforts these past few years. Thank you for being a part of this project by proofreading, providing feedback, and most of all, providing constant support.

Thank you to my amazing book coach, Cathy Fyock. Thank you for encouraging and challenging me, even in the midst of my doubts.

Thank you to the many leaders who contributed to this book in various forms.

I'd also like to thank my amazing editorial board including Gary Carter, Bryan Luci, Terry Dunn, and Scott Buchanan. Thanks to you, this book is stronger and speaks to my reader's needs.

Thank you to all of the colleagues in the various mastermind groups in which I have had a privilege to participate and to my colleagues in the National Speakers Association, especially in the Kentucky chapter.

I also want to thank Everett O'Keefe and his awesome team at Ignite Press for publishing assistance.

TABLE OF CONTENTS

Part 2: Restore Individuals

Part 3: Strengthen Teams

Part 4: Eliminate Gaps

Part 5: Remove Constraints

Introduction

"The dominant hippo male marks his territory
by flinging his dung as far as possible with his tail."
—San Diego Zoo

1

THE ARRIVAL

IT WAS A beautiful morning as the Florida coast slowly unfolded before my eyes. The blue-tinged water mixed with the hum of the airplane engine caused me to tune out the chatter on the radio. I was in my element: in the pilot's seat of a little Piper Warrior airplane on my way to pick up my college roommate and head back to school. The flight back to Virginia would be the culmination of a wonderful, spontaneous trip to the sunshine state over Thanksgiving break, leveraging my new pilot's license.

Five miles out from the airport, I pulled back on the throttle and began my descent. I was all alone and loving it. The air was smooth and the engine was running perfectly as the lakes, rivers, and bays of the coastal lands gradually filled up my windshield. Even better was that my final approach would be over water, landing on what was technically an island. A perfect ending.

Down further now, the plane slipped past the land and continued over the Indian river as I started my final approach. I made my final radio call to let others know I was landing—there was no control tower at this airport. I heard some static on the line but couldn't make it out. No bother—I could see that the runway was clear of any other traffic.

Nearer now, closer to the runway, closer to the water. I stole a peek at the ocean further ahead past the strip of land I was now approaching. Gorgeous. Perhaps I should live down here someday.

Almost there.

My wheels slipped past the river and over the runway at the last moment. I pulled the throttle all the way back and flared to a smooth touchdown.

A fitting end to a memorable flight.

As I pulled off of the active runway and my finger began to depress the button to make my radio call, I paused. Something wasn't right. I pulled myself out of my self-congratulatory reverie and looked around. This is a large airport. I quickly glanced at the chart on my knee. Much larger than the chart indicates. Strange. Is that a second runway over there? Another quick glance down—no, this airport shouldn't have a second runway. Odd. A small knot appeared in my stomach as my brain was trying to put this conflicting information together.

Then, I looked further afield, and my eyes focused on the extra-large words painted on the extra-large hangar building: Patrick Air Force Base.

I gulped. That knot just got a lot bigger.

I was at the wrong destination. And there would be a consequence to pay.

2
THE CONSEQUENCE

THIS BOOK IS for every leader who must navigate their organization to a new destination: a new strategic direction, an important change, a key initiative, a different future.

Reaching that destination is not a solo affair, as I demonstrated on that fateful Florida morning. Instead, the ability for leaders to get their teams, departments, and divisions working *together* without territorial thinking is the key to reaching that destination quickly and successfully. It is just as important as wonderful plans, technical knowledge, stellar strategy, or top-notch skills. Most organizations have good plans, strategies, and skills. Few of them have the organizational teamwork to execute them quickly and at a level high enough to consistently succeed and outmaneuver their competition. My hope for this book is to change that.

Of course, actually getting teams to work together is not so simple in today's world where everything seems important, market conditions change overnight, new opportunities suddenly present themselves, new technologies change the game, new competitors emerge, key personnel change midstream, poor results demand action, or a new regulation, a new law, a new direction, a new executive, a pandemic, or any myriad of other factors distract us from working together to reach the destination. *Forbes Magazine* calls this living in a world of VUCA (Volatility, Uncertainty, Complexity, and Ambiguity).

However, the real issues lie within: territorial thinking, destructive politics, confusion, lack of strategic alignment. These issues destroy the ability of teams and departments to work together, which destroys the ability for organizations to execute at a high level, adapt quickly to changing conditions, and implement their strategies effectively.

It's not just me saying it. PricewaterhouseCoopers reports that only twenty-five percent of executives believe their organization shares information well. *Harvard Business Review* calls us-versus-them thinking a "corrosive problem" and names organizational silos as one of the biggest hurdles to transformation. Deloitte reports that only seventeen percent of C-suite executives regularly collaborate outside their narrow tower of responsibility. In his book *Silos, Politics, and Turf Wars*, Patrick Lencioni said that "silos devastate organizations, kill productivity, and jeopardize the achievement of goals."

The ability for leaders to get their teams, departments, and divisions working together without territorial thinking is the key to reaching the destination quickly and successfully.

This reverberates with my own journey working with several hundred organizations as an employee and consultant, originally in the operations world. Every one of these organizations had a new destination it was seeking, a change that it needed, a future it desired.

There was the engineering company that needed to improve their product delivery; the state government that needed to change their workplace culture, attract new talent, and serve its customers better; the technology division that needed to streamline how they delivered their services; the research and development division that needed to align everyone around new products; the bank that needed to strategically roll out new branches and products; the non-profit that was losing members; the government agency that needed to compete with outside services companies; the church that needed to figure out how to engage a new generation and tackle tough cultural challenges; the supply chain division that needed to deliver consistent performance across their network. And the list goes on.

Despite the varied "destinations," the consistent theme was that too many of these organizations either:

1. Reached a destination, only to discover it wasn't the desired one, much like my flight that fateful morning. The result just didn't meet the needs of the business as envisioned. And so it was scrapped, tolerated, or fixed.
2. Reached the destination, but the journey was marked with multiple deviations, up and down drafts, and sometimes gut-wrenching, vomit-inducing turbulence. People left, trust was lost, and burnout was rampant.
3. Never reached the destination. They crashed, turned back, or gave up and went someplace else. Sometimes they never even got off the ground. Priorities continuously shifted or were not clearly aligned in the first place. Sometimes the project was managed poorly—more often, competing agendas destroyed any hope of success.

In most cases, it was that natural territorial thinking that prevented teams from working together to reach the destination successfully.

That is why this book is called The *Hippo* Solution and why my company is called *Hippo* Solutions. Sure, "hippo" may be a fun name—and I like to have fun—but did you know that hippos are one of the most territorial, hostile animals on the planet? Their nature is aggressive and unpredictable, not unlike some teams and departments tasked with creating critical, even tectonic shifts within an organization. Hippos require careful, sustained energy to navigate around and are an apt metaphor. Going further, there is some "hippo" in all of us—it is a natural tendency to focus on our own goals, our own needs, our own ambitions.

Consider the following statements that I continue to hear almost verbatim from leaders and managers at all levels of organizations of multiple sizes and various industries:

- "We have all sorts of requirements, mandates, initiatives, and programs. Getting everyone to align with each other is really difficult."
- "We don't understand what other departments are doing."
- "It's hard for us to eliminate the disconnects between groups."
- "I wish there were a better way to break the tie."
- "The divide between what one department wants and the rest is very stark on any given day."
- "We have continual conversations that relate to collaborating together. Much of our frustration comes from the gaps between us at some level."

In today's world, teams, departments, and divisions must work together. It's time to eliminate territorial thinking, destructive politics, and confusion. It's time to address the hippos.

3

THE CHALLENGE

THE NEED FOR organizational teamwork—where multiple teams across the organization work together cohesively—is receiving more and more attention. Deloitte reports that C-Suite executives are being asked to work more collaboratively across functions as their roles and work are becoming more complex and integrated and now that we are experiencing a shift from traditional structures to a collaborative "network of teams" structure. *Harvard Business Review* reports that while teams are more "diverse, dispersed, digital, and dynamic," their success depends on group collaboration. General Stanley McChrystal, in his book *Team of Teams*, preaches the necessity of a "team of teams" approach to organizational success in a now-complex world. Patrick Lencioni has started a movement with his Organizational Health model focused on cohesiveness, clarity, and alignment.

Many executives have expressed what Ralph Perrey, Executive Director of the Tennessee Housing Development Agency, expressed to me: They are launching more and more initiatives that require multiple business units to work together.

This is the very job of the leader. The world of work is changing from personal to team performance. It's time for leaders to take this shift seriously.

We don't have to look far to see high-profile examples of leaders doing this well.

Alan Mulally, the former CEO of Boeing Commercial Airplanes and Ford Motor Company, widely credited with turning around the fortunes of Ford, has a very simple model for creating a successful organization. It's called...Working Together.

The world of work is changing from personal to team performance. It's time for leaders to take this shift seriously.

How do you follow in the footsteps of a legend and icon like Steve Jobs? Tim Cook, the CEO of Apple, took on that difficult task and has made Apple even more successful. Cook is known for... focusing on collaboration.

General Stanley McChrystal credits teamwork—not skills or strategy or military doctrine—with the success of his mission against ISIS. If an Army general whose entire career was steeped in a command-and-control model can embrace the importance of organizational teamwork, we should take notice.

Yet for all of the successes from the likes of leaders such as Alan Mulally, Tim Cook, and General McChrystal, there are many failures—even when we implement a particular practice that made those leaders successful. As innovation expert Stephen Shapiro says, we can learn as much from our failures as from our successes. This book is about uncovering truths from both.

Many years ago, I found myself sitting across the table from the civilian director of a command in the Department of Defense, who framed the question perfectly. This gentleman had a wonderful vision to take his organization to the next level, become more effective, and deliver world-class services to their "customers." He wanted to effectively compete with their private sector counterparts. It was both bold and critical to their future funding and existence. Not only did he have a clear vision, like many of the readers of this book, he had a plan to get there.

My role was to provide the software that would drive and coordinate their operations—their delivery projects. As I was sitting there, impressed by his vision, he expressed some of the frustrations he had with the hundreds of people and multiple directorates (departments) who had to carry the vision forward. His frustration was centered around getting all of those directorates both on board and working in unison to achieve his vision.

He finally turned to me and said, "Mark, why is this so difficult?"

His question stopped me in my tracks and changed the trajectory of my career. Indeed, why is working together so difficult?

Let's be honest. Organizational teamwork is important but complicated. There is a reason why organizational teamwork is frustratingly rare. We are dealing with all the intricacies and nuances of human nature, departmental priorities, organizational systems, and complex processes.

The natural tendency is for us-versus-them and territorial thinking to emerge—like a hippo marking its territory.

This all reminds me of the challenges of coaching a basketball team—one of my passions. Any good coach will tell you that an unyielding, unrelenting commitment to teamwork is

> *His question stopped me in my tracks and changed the trajectory of my career. Indeed, why is working together so difficult?*

important. Yet, it is very difficult to develop the level of teamwork required to be successful. Once the girls get in an actual game, when the speed picks up, when the pressure increases, when the environment becomes more intense, when there are consequences, the girls naturally narrow their focus to the immediate individual situation on the court. It can be difficult in an intense game environment for the players to even see their other teammates on the court, much less work together with them.

The secret I discovered is that developing teamwork on the basketball court takes a lot of work and emphasis along *multiple dimensions*. As a coach, you can't just talk about teamwork, you have to develop each individual girl's ball handling and passing skills; each girl has to be able to handle the stress and pressure of a game environment. Team members have to understand how to move in the gaps on the court, passing needs to become stellar, the offensive system needs to adapt to support their strengths— everyone needs to be committed to the same team goal.

What I have discovered is that the secret to developing teamwork on the basketball court is also what it takes to develop teamwork on the organizational "court." It takes a constant emphasis and consistent effort along *multiple dimensions.*

This book will seek to answer the question "Why is this so difficult?" by presenting a multi-dimensional approach centered around five variables, five transformative actions, and one formula. These variables are derived from lessons learned while working with the many organizations with whom I have had the privilege of serving, punctuated with truths from giants in the field of organizational teamwork. The variables, along with their key actions, are set in a formula to demonstrate how they work together to impact organizational teamwork. My hope is that you will think multi-dimensionally about organizational teamwork, understand where the problem lies in your organization, take action right now on one of the variables, and relentlessly commit to making it happen—just like I do with my basketball team and what many successful leaders have already done.

4

THE FIVE VARIABLES

WHEN I FIRST fell in love with airplanes, I would literally stand at the airport fence, watch what was occurring on the other side, and dream about flying. I was enthralled by the magic of flight. I did not study or have an in-depth understanding of the variables that enabled an airplane to fly. I didn't need to. I simply loved and enjoyed the fact that they could.

When I decided to get on the other side of the fence and pursue flight training, that changed. It was important that I understood the whys and hows of flight so that I could both be an effective pilot and always keep the airplane flying.

It's the same with organizational teamwork. When you become a leader, it is important that you understand the factors that affect organizational teamwork—the variables that impact how teams work together across the organization.

The variables are:

1. **The Destination**: the specific, measurable goal of the organization; the future to which the organization is navigating.
2. **The Individuals**: the individual leaders, managers, and team members that make the individual decisions and exhibit the individual behaviors that ultimately determine how teams will work together.
3. **The Teams**: the individual teams, both traditional and non-traditional, where most work gets done today.
4. **The Gaps**: the gaps between the teams, departments, and divisions where information-sharing and working together must take place.
5. **The Constraints**: the five organizational constraints that naturally hinder the ability of teams to work together.

If your teams are not working together across boundaries, the reason will be one or more of these variables. For example, you may have a strong culture of teamwork, but if those teams do not have a clear, collective picture of where the organization is heading, they will have difficulty working together.

Of course, what unlocks the potential of each of the variables is not just understanding them but taking transformative action...

5
THE FIVE TRANSFORMATIVE ACTIONS

NATURALLY, UNDERSTANDING THE variables is not enough. You must take action. There are five transformative actions where the magic occurs—where the power of teams is unleashed across the organization. Without these key actions, the organization remains mired in territorial thinking.

The five transformative actions to create organizational teamwork are:

1. **Simplify the Destination**: Teams are besieged with complexity, contradictions, and confusion about what is

actually important; the specific, measurable destination must be made simple and clear so there is no ambiguity by anyone, anywhere.

2. **Restore Individuals**: Each individual leader, manager, and team member needs to be restored to peak performance, to embrace their calling, and to re-engage in this age of unrelenting stress, pressure, and change.

3. **Strengthen Teams**: Each individual team, both traditional and non-traditional, needs to become high-functioning and cohesive.

4. **Eliminate Gaps**: The gaps between multiple teams need to be eliminated so that information flows freely and teams readily work together to reach the destination.

5. **Remove Constraints**: You must remove the organizational constraints that naturally hinder the ability of teams to work together.

Once leaders recognize where the challenge actually lies, this becomes much simpler. When I speak in front of conference audiences and conduct an impromptu self-assessment, it quickly becomes plain as to which variable requires our energy. At that point, it's a simple matter of focusing energy and action on the correct variable.

In addition to the variables and the key actions, it's also important to understand how the variables impact each other, which brings us to the formula.

6
THE FORMULA

LEADERS MUST UNDERSTAND not just the variables but how those variables work together to drive organizational teamwork. The formula is:

$$\text{The Destination} \times \frac{\text{Individuals} \times \text{Teams} \times \text{Gaps}}{\text{Organizational Constraints}}$$

When you improve the variables on the top of the formula—individuals, teams, and gaps—it multiplies and unleashes teamwork throughout the organization. The constraints variable divides and negates the ability for teams to work together. A simple, clear, actionable destination shared by everyone in the organization activates the entire formula.

It's a simple formula, but that doesn't mean it's easy. It takes discipline and work to create organizational teamwork.

Throughout the rest of this book, we will walk through each variable and provide simple actions to take right now so that you can arrive at the proper destination every time. By the time you are finished, you will know where to focus your energy and what action to take. Let's begin with the first variable and key action.

As you read this book, visit TheHippoSolution.com/bookresources for assessments, downloads, and additional resources.

Part 1
Simplify the Destination

"Hippos are highly aggressive and considered
one of the most dangerous animals in Africa,
particularly if you get between the hippo
and its destination: the water."
—Kariega Game Reserve

$$\textbf{THE DESTINATION} \times \frac{\textbf{Individuals} \times \textbf{Teams} \times \textbf{Gaps}}{\textbf{Organizational Constraints}}$$

7

TURNING AROUND A POINT

AS I TRAINED for my pilot's license, there were many maneuvers in which I had to become proficient. Some of the maneuvers I tolerated but did not particularly enjoy. For example, I didn't care for steep turns. Turning the airplane and banking the wings 45 degrees so that it felt like you were looking straight at the ground was a little disconcerting.

But there was one maneuver that I always enjoyed: turning around a point.

The concept is simple enough. You pick a reference point on the ground and circle all the way around it. The goal is to stay exactly the same distance from the reference point at all times—never closer, never farther away, while maintaining the same altitude.

The first time I attempted the maneuver, my instructor was in the right seat as we took off and flew to the practice area. He looked out the window and pointed to a red house in the middle of a field.

"See that red house?"

"Yes," I replied.

"Use that as your reference point and turn around it, just like we talked about."

"Okay."

I focused on the house. When we were adjacent to it, I turned the yoke in order to bank the plane to the left and start my turn. I made some minor adjustments as we began to circle around the house. So far so good. All the way around the house, it was the same thing. This was easy.

I finished up the turn. My instructor gave me a simple "nice job" but didn't say too much beyond that. Okay, then.

We completed a couple more turns and then moved on to some other maneuvers. No problem. Check that box.

Two days later, we went up to practice maneuvers again, and my instructor repeated himself.

"See that yellow barn down there? Use that as your reference point and turn around it."

When we were adjacent to the barn, I started my turn. So far, so good. I got this.

A little adjustment here, a little adjustment there... Hey, wait a minute, what's happening? We were suddenly pushed farther away. I had to bank at a steeper angle to correct for our drift and bring us back to the right distance from the barn.

Okay, that's better. Now just continue to... whoa! There it goes again. What... on... Earth... is... happening?

The wind! Of course! Today, the wind had picked up. It was playing with my ego and making it harder to stay in a perfect circle.

I quickly glanced over at my instructor just in time to catch the smirk on his face. He was enjoying this learning experience.

I spent the entire turn adjusting my bank angle—steeper, now shallower, now steeper again—while constantly watching my altitude but failing to stay in a perfect circle this time. I needed some practice after all.

Later, I would learn how to read and picture the wind, understand what it's going to do before it did it, be able to predict it, be ready for it, and pro-actively adjust for it instead of simply reacting to it.

The reason it was even possible that I could adjust to the wind was that I had that clear reference point. I always knew if I was on course or off course and what I had to do in order to correct my course.

Your teams need the same thing. They are getting blown around by the wind and need a reference point as simple, clear, distinct, and actionable as the red house in the field.

8

A CONFUSING DESTINATION

WHEN I STARTED off in the IT profession after college, I worked on various projects and initiatives to support the organization, many of which were our own interpretations of what we thought the organization needed. I couldn't possibly look back and tell you the goals of the organization. I couldn't have told you the goals even when I worked there. Our department launched initiatives. Those initiatives helped us do our job better and serve our internal customers more effectively. For many companies, this may be adequate, but don't you want more? This book is for leaders who want more than departments simply doing their jobs well in isolation.

We all have a vision—where we want the organization to be in the future, what we want it to accomplish, how we want it to impact the world. It's our desired destination. Perhaps it is centered around growth, repositioning, launching, diversifying, making a difference, or just surviving. If you're like me, you even have an emotional investment in achieving your vision.

While the vision—the destination—may be clear to the leader, for many teams, the destination is complex, confusing, or even contradictory. They do not understand where the organization is heading, how it will get there, and how their team can directly contribute. This is a major reason why teams develop territorial thinking and don't work together.

This book is for leaders who want more than departments simply doing their jobs well in isolation.

I consistently witness three mistakes:

The first mistake is that leaders over-complicate. There is too much verbiage, or they create pages and pages of complicated strategic plans or a long list of strategic priorities that no one can remember or legitimately act upon, much less work together to accomplish.

In 2006, when Alan Mulally took over at Ford Motor Company, Ford was in trouble. It would be a complex undertaking to turn it around. *Forbes Magazine* gave significant credit to Alan Mulally for his ability to frame the complex issues and concepts quickly and simply. Mulally created a "One Ford" plan that fit onto a business card.

Likewise, your success will not be predicated on your ability to create complex plans but on your ability to simplify, both in the strategy and the communication of the strategy. Simplifying is what distinguishes great leaders.

The second mistake is that leaders don't decide what's actually important. This typically plays out as a long list of "equally important" priorities, which most people do not remember. They fall prey to the false belief that in order to be successful, they must accomplish a great many things.

Most of the organizations with whom I consult are busier than ever and trying so hard to "do more with less." Popular innovation expert and author Stephen Shapiro lays bare the fallacy of this thinking in his book *Invisible Solutions*. Instead of "doing more with less," organizations need to "do less, get more." The leaders who are able to focus their organizations on the activities that most move the needle are the leaders who are able to make their product or service amazing, capture the market, and "get more."

The third mistake is that there is no effective system of cascading what is actually important to every level of the organization. Teams may understand the strategy but are confused as to how they should be contributing to achieve the strategy.

These mistakes are evidenced by numerous studies, such as PricewaterhouseCoopers reporting that "strong and clear messaging from the C-Suite" is sorely lacking in many organizations and MIT reporting that only twenty-eight percent of executives and middle managers can list even three of their company's strategic priorities.

Leaders must make the destination simple, clear, distinct, and actionable so that there is no ambiguity by anyone, anywhere. The distinct destination must be as clear as the reference point was to me during my flight training: the red house in the field.

When your teams and departments are confused or have even the slightest level of ambiguity, they have to make up their own reference point based on their own interpretation of what's important. That makes it much more difficult for them to work together at all levels as you need them to do. They are not navigating to the same place.

This doesn't mean that there is no complexity in the organization or its initiatives. It means that there is no complexity or ambiguity in the actual definition of the destination.

When your teams and departments are confused or have even the slightest level of ambiguity, they make up their own reference point based on their own interpretation of what's important. That makes it much more difficult for them to work together at all levels as you need them to do. They are not navigating to the same place.

The problem here is that most leadership teams think they are providing a distinct destination—a clear reference point for everyone. To the teams that need to execute it, however, the destination is anything but clear. This is because:

1. The leadership team thinks the reference point is clear in their own minds, but it is not clear to anyone else, or
2. The leadership team is conflicted and not cohesively committed to a single, clear reference point. They have multiple reference points, or
3. The leadership team has a clear reference point but has not effectively and continuously communicated it.

Laura Paluch is a Senior R&D Director who has built and managed R&D teams for multiple companies over the years. According to Paluch, when launching new initiatives that require resources from other functions, "They may not have the same belief that what you want to do next is the right thing to do." For example, her research and development team may believe that it's the right thing to launch this new product, whereas the manufacturing team may not agree because it will upset their existing product lines and tooling, or a global entity may try to push a new product initiative that isn't accepted by regional entities because they are focused on their profit and loss. "You have to understand where senior leaders sit in terms of wanting certain projects to move forward. You have to get that buy-in first before moving forward," says Paluch.

When the goal and direction were aligned at a higher level, her job was much easier because everyone had the same clear goal—the same reference point.

But when that reference point is not there, when clarity is not provided at a higher level, it's much harder for directors at her level to build alignment with other groups because everyone then has their own goals and agendas.

This captures what it's like throughout the organization when there is the slightest level of ambiguity from higher up in the organization. Every group is busy navigating to a different destination.

9

THE MODEL

ONE OF THE major reasons that I landed at the Air Force base was that my intended destination—my reference point—was ambiguous. I was looking for an airport along the coast that was on an island that bordered the ocean, was across a river from the mainland, and on a 109-degree heading from Orlando Executive Airport.

That description sounds pretty specific and distinct, doesn't it? It wasn't. It turns out there is another airport just a few miles south that was on an island along the coast, across a river, with a runway in the same direction. The way I defined my destination didn't work: It was too ambiguous. Unfortunately, that ambiguity landed me in hot water.

When I consult with senior leadership teams, they often have established a set of strategic priorities and perhaps inspirational mission and vision statements for the organization. In my own experience, this approach falls short when departments focus exclusively on the priorities that apply to them, constrained resources have to decide which strategic priority is more important, and teams on the front lines are given a series of milestones that are equally important. The result is that teams do not work together across departments, progress on important strategic initiatives is slow, and teams get burned out because everything is important.

Leaders and teams need more than a list of strategic priorities. They need three distinct points of clarity: a three-pronged approach.

When flying, I would take my bearings from three known sources. The intersection of those three bearings would give me an exact position, both of my destination and of my current location. If I had utilized this technique, called triangulation, I would never have accidentally landed at the Air Force base on that morning in Florida.

In organizations, utilizing a three-pronged approach will do the same thing for your teams. It provides bearings from three known sources. These bearings give teams throughout the organization a simple, clear, distinct, actionable destination so every team is navigating to the same place. There is no ambiguity. I call this "Organizational Triangulation." Organizational Triangulation is how you make the destination simple and actionable.

Before we look at the three bearings, we must make an important clarification. This effort is all about helping your teams work together across the organization to go "someplace." That "someplace" may be a big ambition for the organization, like privatizing space travel, or becoming the market leader, or solving a big problem, or disrupting a market. We're not talking about staying where we are currently. I worked for years in roles where I was helping organizations become more efficient or implement better processes. That's great. That is all part of the process of continuing normal, daily operations. That is necessary and, of course, teams are going to spend time and energy keeping daily operations going.

The problem is when teams *only* work on keeping up with daily operations. Teams do this because they have no insight into where leaders are leading the organization and which activities the team needs to prioritize in order to get there. For example, a team may be working on daily manufacturing activities, but it may be important, critical even, for them to actually focus on improving the quality of those activities. That would be important if, for example, the organization has a current goal of greatly improving their reputation in the marketplace. If the three-pronged approach is not put into place, this won't happen—or it will take much longer to permeate the goal throughout the organization.

In order for organizations to change faster, to implement strategic direction more effectively, to fulfill a significant purpose, they need to become, as General McChrystal puts it, one "team of teams." The key that activates that process is to first have a simple, clear definition of the destination. Everyone needs to know where the organization is going and how they can contribute to reaching it. The three organizational bearings model is an easy model to make this happen.

I am walking on the shoulders of giants here: Stephen Covey, John Maxwell, Patrick Lencioni, Jim Collins, and many, many others. There have been many great books and resources on the topic of organizational teamwork and execution, many of which are mentioned in these pages and leveraged when I work with senior leadership teams. Despite all of these resources, despite our best efforts, confusion still reigns in so many teams at multiple levels, creating territorial thinking and a barrier to working together. My goal is to provide a new way of thinking about organizational direction to eliminate confusion while leveraging the truths from these great organizational thinkers. Specifically, my goal is to provide a model to provide clear direction in three dimensions. It is not one piece of information that teams need in order to understand direction—it is three. Most leaders miss this and wonder why teams are not working together to achieve the direction. Hence, the three-pronged approach.

The three organizational bearings every team in every organization needs identified are:

Bearing #1: The Ultimate Ambition

of the organization

The leadership team must provide the clear ambition of the organization on which every other decision is based.

Bearing #2: The Current Goal

of the organization

The leadership team must provide a single, short-term, big goal for the organization.

Bearing #3: The Immediate Objective

of every team

Each individual team needs to have its own immediate objective that is *most important* to help the organization achieve its big goal.

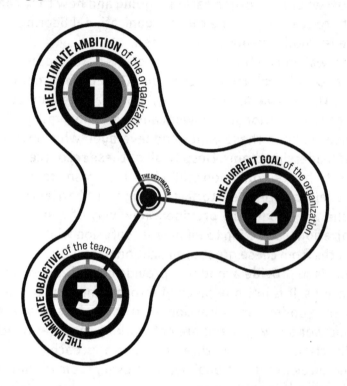

When teams do not understand the **Ultimate Ambition** of the organization, decisions about strategy and work priorities are made across the organization on a whim without the foundation of what is ultimately driving the organization. Teams will make their own strategic choices because they don't know what is ultimately important. Worse, they won't make any choices because they have no basis on which to make them and don't want to make the wrong choice. There is no foundational purpose and strategy on which to rally. This causes a retreat into territorial thinking.

When teams do not have a collective **Current Goal** to rally around, every department and function decides for themselves what is currently important or, more common, everything becomes important. This reaction again causes a retreat into territorial thinking—focusing on one's own department or group priorities.

When teams do not have their own related **Immediate Objective**, the chaos of everyday work takes over. Teams get lost in the madness of the everyday because they are missing a consistent focus on what's going to most move the needle for the organization. As a result, progress on the organization's most important initiative is slow. Energy is wasted. Teams don't see themselves as contributing to the organization's strategy. Yet again, they retreat into territorial thinking—focusing on their own everyday tasks.

I want you to recognize that all three bearings are critical in order to eliminate territorial thinking and unleash your teams.

Once again, this does not mean that teams will not work on any other objectives. Of course they will. It does mean that everyone understands what is most important right now in order for the organization to achieve its ambition, because as Patrick Lencioni is fond of saying, "If everything is important, nothing is important." There is great power when a leadership team embraces this truth.

Let's look at a well-known, if overused, example.

Look at NASA in the 1960s. NASA was an incredibly large and complex organization, but the destination was clear. There was the Ultimate Ambition: land a man on the moon and return him safely. For a decade, every single person knew it and could articulate that ambition, despite the size, scope, and vast complexity of the organization. Think about the power of that for a moment. This clarity was the catalyst to focus the best of the resources and energy of hundreds of thousands of people.

There was always a Current Goal, at various points in time, that was big and clear. It may have been starting the Gemini program or the Apollo program or correcting safety issues or a particular launch or mission objective.

Every team had an Immediate Objective to support NASA's Current Goal. It may have been to design and test the flight computer or to develop mission control rules. Every team had clear focus on what work it had to accomplish in order to achieve NASA's Current Goal and Ultimate Ambition. There was no ambiguity about where the organization was heading and how their team would contribute.

By teams achieving their Immediate Objectives over time, which helped achieve the Current Goals over time, NASA eventually achieved its Ultimate Ambition on July 24, 1969, with the return of Apollo 11.

That's the power that leaders unleash when they make the destination simple, clear, distinct, and actionable. Teams have a reason to work together. You start to unleash the power of teams.

This model can be used to lead at any level. Whether you lead an entire company, a board, a department, a division, or a function, that organization needs an Ultimate Ambition, a Current Goal, and Immediate Team Objectives.

Now that you are thinking with a three-pronged approach, let's look at how to put in place each bearing. The good news is that we don't have to recreate the wheel. There are excellent models that we can leverage for a three-pronged approach that activates every team.

10

BEARING #1: THE AMBITION OF THE ORGANIZATION

EARLY ONE MORNING while running at a nearby park, something caught my eye as I came out into a clearing. Another runner. My interest immediately piqued—while there are usually several people walking their dog, there are typically not many people running this early in the morning.

My leisurely, average-paced jog in the park had suddenly turned into something else: I was going to catch up to this fellow runner.

My pace picked up, my heart rate picked up, my intensity picked up, my enthusiasm picked up, even my knees picked up as I focused in on my fellow runner.

There is something special that happens when the bar has been raised, when there is something bigger to accomplish, when everyone knows that achieving it comes with a level of satisfaction when you know exactly what you must achieve and exactly how to achieve it.

Knowing the Ultimate Ambition of the organization does exactly that. It is not simply creating and regurgitating a mission or vision statement or publishing a five-year plan or a list of strategic priorities. It goes far beyond that. It is understanding why the organization exists, how the organization will operate, where it is going, how it will be successful. Perhaps most importantly, it tells people what the organization is not. Everyone must know the Ambition. Not only does it provide clarity, it provides an aspiring future to attain. It also attracts top talent and motivates your current talent to stay.

There is something special that happens when the bar has been raised, when there is something bigger to accomplish, when everyone knows that achieving it comes with a level of satisfaction, when you know exactly what you must achieve and exactly how to achieve it.

Pixar was the creator of animated hits like *Toy Story*, *A Bug's Life*, and *Cars*, but it started with the ambition of creating the first computer-animated feature film. Everyone aspired to achieve that ambition.

Employees at Southwest Airlines are able to take action in the moment because they both understand and are empowered to help the airline be on time, have low fares, and create loyal customers—the three distinct strategies that make the airline successful. Employees understand what sets the airline apart.

GE's business units became the first or second in their respective industries, or they would no longer be a part of GE.

The model that I typically use when consulting with senior leadership teams is Patrick Lencioni's organization clarity model from his book *The Advantage*. I love this model because it is simple and yet forces leadership teams to wrestle with relevant, meaningful questions. Lencioni's model can be used by any size organization. In this model, Lencioni articulates six questions every leadership team must answer:

1. Why do we exist?: the organization's purpose
2. How do we behave?: the organization's three or four core values
3. What do we do?: the actual business the organization is in
4. How will we succeed?: the three strategies that make the organization successful
5. What is most important right now?: the short-term, most important goal
6. Who must do what?: what action will be taken by whom

When teams throughout the organization have the answers to these questions, it grounds them, gives them a reason to work together, and raises the bar. Think about the power of having an ambition of landing a man on the moon or making space travel routine or eliminating a disease or raising people out of poverty or launching a new technology or disrupting a market. Teams want to work together to achieve

The problem is when leadership teams never take the time to uncover differing opinions and perceptions and do the work to create real alignment instead of faux alignment.

that type of ambition. By understanding the answers to the questions, teams know the purpose as well as the specifics of how they will succeed in achieving it. That is powerful.

Answering these questions is not as easy as it sounds. There are almost always unexpected differing opinions on the leadership team around the answers to the key questions. The problem is not when there are differing opinions. The problem is when leadership teams never take the time to uncover differing opinions and perceptions and do the work to create real alignment instead of faux alignment. This is their job.

Go to the book resource page for resources on implementing Lencioni's model. We don't need to cover all of the details of how to implement the model here. That's already been done in Lencioni's book and other resources. The point here is that your organization is operating on shifting sand if you don't go through the work of creating your organization's Ambition.

If you don't like Lencioni's model, that's fine. There are several fine models that you can leverage to provide your organization a compelling ambition. EOS, The Rockefeller Habits, and Objectives and Key Results come to mind. The point is to go through the work of creating the Ambition. It provides the foundation for everything and everyone in your organization. Without it, your organization is built on shifting sand.

Go to the book resource page for information and resources to adopt one of these models.

Oh, by the way, that runner on the trail? It took two laps, but I caught up to them.

11

BEARING #2: THE CURRENT GOAL OF THE ORGANIZATION

IT'S NOT ENOUGH to be clear about the organization's Ambition. It's also critical to know the Organization's Current Goal. You will not get traction across the organization if there is not one clear, specific, and measurable most important goal for the short term.

This is so simple and yet so hard for many leadership teams. Leadership teams tend to push back on the idea that there is one thing that is currently most important. After all, there are so many objectives that need to be accomplished. These teams miss out on the power of focus. Leaders who are able to focus on one most important goal get more out of their organization. One collective goal creates a guidepost that every team can rally around. It gives those teams a reason to work together: They are all focused on the same collective goal.

Stated differently, if teams do not have a most important collective goal that requires them to work together, they are not going to work together. Why would they?

When I was speaking recently for a group of leaders at a state agency, there was, unsurprisingly, initial hesitation with this concept. We are so conditioned to prioritize many important objectives at once. It wasn't until I demonstrated what having one big current goal really means that light bulbs started to go off.

You will not get traction across the organization if there is not one clear, specific, and measurable most important goal for the short term.

If *you* are still struggling with this concept, consider these two points of clarification.

First, this is not referring to everyday business operations. Will teams work on multiple tasks and projects to keep the business running? Of course they will. The Current Goal is to achieve more—to improve those operations or to launch a new product or to take the next step in the organization's Ultimate Ambition. The Current Goal is the one activity that will most move the needle for the organization. Without it, nothing changes, as teams only focus on the everyday.

> *If teams do not have a most important collective goal that requires them to work together, they are not going to work together.*

Second, the Current Goal may have multiple initiatives or objectives underneath it. For example, the organization's Current Goal may be to open key new locations. Will there be a lot of work and several objectives required to accomplish that goal? Yes, of course. However, no one can rally around "several objectives." They can rally around *one* goal, such as "increase our market share by opening new locations."

Patrick Lencioni once again articulates this nicely in his Thematic Goal model, embedded in his Organization Clarity model: "What is most important right now?" and "Who must do what?"

Another excellent model to define the Current Goal is the 4DX model from Chris McChesney, Sean Covey, and Jim Huling's book, *The 4 Disciplines of Execution*. The 4DX model refers to this as a wildly important goal. The wildly important goal might be launching a new product or merging two businesses or acquiring more market share or improving the quality of products or fixing a hot issue.

Both Lencioni's and the 4DX models break the Current Goal into two parts.

In Lencioni's model, the two parts are the thematic goal statement and the defining objectives that define the goal. He advocates answering the question, "If we accomplish one thing during the next x months, what would it be?"

In the 4DX model, the two parts are the wildly important goal and the lead measures on which to focus in order to achieve it. McChesney, Covey, and Huling advocate answering the question, "If every other area of our operation remained at its current level of performance, what is the one area where change would have the greatest impact?"

Without a Current Goal for the organization, teams across the organization spend enormous energy to align with other teams around a consistent, watered-down but agreeable vision.

Both of these models have one defining goal statement that is simple, clear, and easy to repeat: what I refer to as the Current Goal.

Without a Current Goal for the organization, teams across the organization end up spending enormous energy to align with other teams around a consistent, watered-down but agreeable vision.

Go to the book resource page to download instructions on exactly how to create this goal with your leadership team utilizing Lencioni's or the 4DX model. This can be done quickly—even within a couple of hours—and yields almost immediate benefits.

We'll come back to this when we review the four steps to simplify the destination in your organization.

Let's look at some varied examples of Current Goals.

12

EXAMPLES OF CURRENT GOALS

THE VP OF Engineering of a manufacturing company with whom I worked, transformed his team to the point where project management was known to their customers as the strength of the company. He came into his job and worked with his team to create a project management goal that how they manage and deliver projects to customers is going to be their greatest strength. It was a clear articulation of what's currently most important: In this case, improving how they manage and deliver projects.

When I became President of the Association for Talent Development's Nashville chapter, we didn't want to just do the same things on the board that had been done every year before. That would have been like an average pace around the trail. My President-elect and I created a bold goal with the board: to create an amazing member experience that year that would result in doubling our membership. Again, the actual goal should be specific: Delivering x programs with x percent satisfaction in the next x number of months.

One of my first jobs was a cook at Pizza Hut. The job of the cook is to take the dough from the refrigerators, swirl pizza sauce and toppings on the dough, and then place it in the oven. That was my job as I understood it. Or was it? About midway through my first summer, "the kitchen" wasn't getting pizzas out to customers fast enough. Our manager told us that our goal was to "get pizzas out to customers in 15 minutes or less." Today, that sounds like a Geico commercial. Back then, it was the Current Goal we needed. We needed to have the intensity, pace, and system to get pizzas out quickly and correctly—not just the cooks but everyone, including the wait staff. And we did.

The goal was so clear that I can remember it more than 30 years later.

When I worked for a manufacturing company in Seattle, our company was focused on achieving ISO certification. There was no ambiguity, even for myself in IT, a department you wouldn't always think of when you think of quality manufacturing systems. Achieving ISO certification by a specific date was our number one job—we were to put in place quality systems, regardless of our department. The executive team created a mantra. The Quality Manager gave out "ISO bucks" whenever he "caught" someone performing a task that contributed to quality. Everyone bought into the effort. I even won a grill through one of the raffles!

The goal was so clear that I can remember it more than 30 years later.

You'll notice that some of these are company examples and some are department or division examples. You can use this model for whichever you are leading.

One of my favorite "rallying" goal statements comes from Darren Harris, the CEO of the Bone and Joint Institute in Franklin, Tennessee. As this brand-new institute opened up, there were naturally a number of "fires," as you would expect if you have ever launched any new business or organization. But Darren and his leadership team didn't want the organization to focus on simply putting out fires. They wanted to solve the source of the fire—to eliminate the systemic issue that caused the fire in the first place. For example, if a scheduling problem arose, instead of just solving that scheduling problem, they wanted to figure out why that scheduling problem occurred in the first place and prevent it from occurring again.

This was what the leadership team determined was the most important focus of the organization for a period of time. As such, they adopted the statement of "take away the matches," meaning find the source of the flame, don't just put out the fire. They even hung a big banner in the break room.

Everyone in the organization knew both what the focus was and understood exactly what it meant. That's a great example of what I'm talking about here.

13

BEARING #3: THE IMMEDIATE OBJECTIVE OF EACH TEAM

THE PROBLEM OF stopping after the first two bearings is that individual teams don't know what it means for them—what they should be doing, if anything. They don't understand their role and contribution. They get sucked into their daily jobs and the never-ending requests for their time. They end up working on initiatives and tasks to keep the business running. Granted, that's important, but it's also vital to be moving forward. That is done by teams throughout the organization also working on what's most important.

You will inevitably fail to get teams working together if you do not add the third bearing: the Immediate Objective for the team.

The organization's Ambition and Current Goal are worthless if teams don't actually make them their own top priority and use them to guide the team's work decisions. While the leadership team creates the organization's Ambition and Current Goal, each team needs to create its own Immediate Objective.

I leave the definition of "team" ambiguous on purpose, as organizations are turning into a web of teams that cross traditional boundaries. A team could be a traditional departmental leadership team, a functional team, a field office team, a project team, a cross-functional team, a task force team. Regardless of the definition of "team," they each need a clear Immediate Objective. The Immediate Objective gives every member of the team a clear picture of how they contribute to the organization's overall Ambition and Current Goal.

The leadership team contributes to this important step in three ways:

1. Insisting that every team create and have their own Immediate Objective for the team that supports the organization's Current Goal. In the 4DX model, the authors advocate that leaders do not create these objectives for teams but can veto them if they do not support the Current Goal.
2. Insisting that every team implement daily and weekly rhythms to keep their objective front and center, starting with the leadership team itself.
3. Insisting that teams regularly brief their immediate leaders on their Immediate Objective, both what the objective is and the progress towards achieving that objective.

Daily and weekly rhythms are the only way to constantly review and focus the team on what's most important every day. Daily check-ins, weekly tactical meetings, and sometimes daily check-outs are critical rhythms to ensure that teams do not get distracted by seemingly important items that in reality distract from what's most important: the team's Immediate Objective.

14

THE TEAM ONE SHEET

THIS FALL, MY wife decided to clean out our garage, which had accumulated too much unnecessary clutter. In the middle of the project, she walked into the house holding a box that was packed and labeled for a garage sale that she planned to have five years ago. It was part of her plan to clear out clutter and make some money in the process. It never happened. The box just sat there for five years.

There's no reason to even go through this exercise if we don't have tools in place to use what is actually most important.

All of these allusions to reference points and destinations and organizational bearings mean nothing unless we actually navigate with them. I could sit in the cockpit of my airplane, have the most accurate bearings, and be clear on my ultimate destination, but if I don't use that information as I navigate, it's worthless. I'll end up at the wrong airport again.

There is no reason to even go through this exercise if we don't have tools in place to use what is actually most important. It's wasted energy.

That's where the Team One Sheet comes in.

The Team One Sheet is a one-page document, unique to each team and carried around by everyone on that team. The document lists the following information:

- The Organization's Ambition: answers to the six questions

- The Organization's Current Goal
- The Team's Immediate Objective, along with green/yellow/red status of pertinent milestones, initiatives, or tasks to achieve that objective, as well as who is responsible for what, by when
- Pertinent objectives to conduct business as usual
- Our expected behaviors
- The specific current focus area to become a more cohesive team (more on this in Part 3: Strengthen Teams)
- Your team's 10-3-2-1 rhythm (more on this in Part 3: Strengthen Teams)

Everyone should pull the Team One Sheet out and refer to it at the start of every meeting. It is the foundation of meetings and the focal point of day-to-day decisions.

Only by utilizing a rhythm tool such as the Team One Sheet can you make significant progress on your most important objective.

Visit the book resource page for a template.

15
FOUR STEPS TO SIMPLIFY YOUR DESTINATION

THE OBJECTIVE IS for every team to be clear on all three organizational bearings. When that occurs, you have simplified the destination for them. They will understand it, know when they've reached it, and most importantly, know what they must do together to help the organization reach it.

Of course, it's not quite that easy. It's not enough to understand the concept of the three organizational bearings or for the leadership team to create the bearings by themselves in a room. We have to follow the right process to create them.

There is a distinct process to create a destination—a clear reference point—that is simple, clear, and distinct. The process has four steps: Create, Absorb, Do, and Adjust. This process can be leveraged regardless of the organizational level in which you lead.

It's not enough to understand the concept of the three organizational bearings or for the leadership team to create the bearings by themselves in a room.
We have to follow the right process to create them.

16
STEP 1: CREATE

THE THREE ORGANIZATIONAL bearings must first be created, starting with the first two bearings: the Organization's Ultimate Ambition and its Current Goal.

Naturally, this is the job of the senior leadership team.

The first bearing—the Ambition of the Organization—is best created through a strategic working retreat when the leadership team can get away from the chaos of the everyday. This may sound like a lot of time until you realize that your entire organization is drifting until you establish it. That sounds pretty important to me, and it's time well spent.

The second bearing, the Current Goal of the Organization, can be created at the same time.

When I facilitate strategic working retreats with senior leadership teams, they are fast-moving sessions to get real work done around team cohesiveness, meeting effectiveness, and organizational alignment. Done right, your team—and by extension, your organization—will not be the same afterward.

Both of these bearings need to be constantly reviewed, though the first bearing doesn't change as much.

The second organizational bearing—the Current Goal—changes regularly as goals are achieved. It requires constant attention.

Make sure that you don't create these bearings in a vacuum without the entire leadership team. If you have a conflicted leadership team or it's just one executive dictating direction, which is not uncommon, it will be very difficult for teams to work together because they will be receiving conflicting messages from different members of the leadership team. Just the other week, I heard yet another retelling of this saga: a team where the sole executive made all of the decisions, creating a lack of commitment, cohesion, and alignment that rippled through the organization.

Tip: If you need to develop clarity quickly with limited time, start by creating a current most important goal for the organization. That can be done in a couple of hours and has immediate benefits.

You may be wondering if you should engage other people and teams from the rest of the organization in the process. The answer is yes, but not yet. For one thing, it's the leadership team's responsibility to ultimately set the direction. For another, I find that it's quicker and more effective for the leadership team to create a direction to which others can react.

At that point, you can engage others in the process. That brings us to step two.

17
STEP 2: ABSORB

THE VERY FIRST time I prepared the airplane to embark on a solo cross-country flight, I felt a mixture of excitement and nervousness. It was a clear, sunny day. I was going to fly this plane, navigate to two different airports, each more than 50 miles away, and navigate back, all by myself. It was a pretty cool feeling.

I completed my flight plan and took my gear to the airplane. I eschewed a full weather briefing because the whole region had great weather.

As soon as I took off and climbed to a safe altitude, I started navigating. There's the lake. Right on course. About 15 minutes later, I found my second checkpoint, the highway and railroad tracks. Excellent. So far, so good. I let myself relax a little bit.

Wait… What was that up ahead? Clouds? Where did they come from? Hopefully, the clouds would be high enough that it wouldn't affect my flight. I wasn't qualified to fly through the clouds, but I could fly beneath them—provided there was plenty of room to be safe.

There wasn't. Maybe I should have obtained that full weather briefing after all.

I ended up turning back. I'd have to try again another day.

The problem was that while I had created a plan, I stopped there. I assumed that the weather would be fine throughout the entire course. It wasn't. What I should have done was take a little extra time to get a full weather briefing. I would have known about the clouds along my route, and I could have changed my course to navigate around them or even changed my destination.

That extra step would have saved a lot of time and money, as it will for you with your teams.

You can't stop at creating the bearings and just expect that they will be executed flawlessly. They won't.

It's much better to take some time and let your organization absorb the direction and change. Even just a few days draws out issues that are much easier dealt with now.

This is where I disagree with some consultants who would say that the leadership team needs to just set the direction and communicate it to the organization. Certainly, if the leadership team has no desire to actually hear and implement feedback, that is what they should do: set the direction and move forward. However, there are valid reasons to learn the discipline of allowing the organization to absorb the direction. You are not giving people the power of vetoing the direction—only allowing time to absorb and provide feedback into the direction. The reasons to do this include:

1. *It is important for people to understand not just the change itself but the intent behind the change.* That helps them make better decisions later on when implementing the change.

2. *The people on the front lines generally know better how things work and can identify roadblocks now.* They will provide feedback that will make the change more realistic and help you think about issues and perspectives that you haven't thought of yet. That's really important. You'll encounter these issues eventually, so you might as well address them now.

3. *It creates an environment of co-creating.* They are a part of this. We're doing this together. Michael Stallard, in his book *Connection Culture*, strongly suggests adopting an attitude of co-creating to prevent us-versus-them attitudes and more importantly for everyone to feel connected together to the strategy.

4. *It gives teams the opportunity to create their own Immediate Objective* and receive confirmation that it truly supports the organization's goal.

5. *It allows time to anticipate and tackle defensive behaviors.* In essence, you are asking teams to behave differently. *Harvard Business Review* emphasizes that you have to anticipate how they will experience the request. If teams see the request as de-legitimizing their importance or responsibilities or think that they will no longer be needed, true or not, teams will put up barriers and intentionally resist collaboration. Taking the time to absorb allows you to look for and tackle these responses upfront, perhaps by emphasizing the group's importance, clarifying their identity, or expanding their control over certain areas. It's better to address these now rather than when they come up in the middle of the journey.

Without involving people on the front lines, you create frustration and low morale, not to mention losing the ability to anticipate problems that will naturally arise.

Without involving people on the front lines, you create frustration and low morale, not to mention losing the ability to anticipate problems that will naturally arise.

Colin Callahan, Chief Executive Officer of Acklen Avenue, describes his approach to creating clarity together with the teams in their organization: "I always make sure that I am setting the context in a way that they know I'm not coming to this meeting as 'the boss' or that 'this is the way it is going to be.' Instead, we are going to have a discussion about it and come up with the best solution together."

After creating this context, Colin finds that decisions become organic. After talking it through, it becomes apparent that "Yeah, this is what we should do."

It's part of creating an environment that brings out the best in people and allows them to thrive.

18
ABSORBING IN ACTION

HOW DO YOU actually let your people absorb the goals? Go out there and talk to people. Have two-way conversations. Don't just send out company-wide emails or videos. Go out and have real conversations with real people. Here are some specific examples.

1. Conduct Knowledge Flow Sessions: Michael Stallard advocates for sitting down with a small group of people—what he refers to as a Knowledge Flow Session. Share the vision and ask them what's right, what's wrong, and what's missing. Then sit back, ask questions, and listen. I was reluctant to add this suggestion because it can backfire. If you're just there to go through the motions, don't bother. Frontline workers will sniff this out in a second. But if you're sincerely interested in learning what's missing, what's right and what's wrong with your thinking, and what you're not considering, then it is of real benefit. But don't give any BS like you're going to use all of their suggestions. Tell them the truth. Just point out what you learned, what you will sincerely consider, and thank them. Too many companies pretend to listen.

2. Spend One-on-One Time: Do the same thing one-on-one with every one of your leaders/direct reports and preferably some of the people underneath them. Ask the same questions. It is time well spent. Not only will people

understand the direction, they can begin to understand the intent behind it.

3. Hold Informal "Date Nights": Tim Cook, CEO of Apple, is well known for holding "Date Nights with Tim" where he would go to a department on a Friday and just talk with folks, sometimes well into the evening. Holding these types of sessions builds relationships, communicates goals and intent, and provides valuable feedback.

4. "Neighborhood" Halls: I don't like "town halls" as much because they are big and often ineffective unless you are really skilled at navigating a large crowd. I like "Neighborhood" Halls with smaller groups of people. Let people ask whatever they want to ask about the direction or a particular goal. Answer them the best you can. Don't hide information. Kris Kelso, author of *Overcoming the Imposter*, advocates for being direct, honest, and clear, even and especially during difficult times. Be honest and transparent. Think "listen" more than "talk."

5. Provide a Constant Feedback Mechanism: Team members need a channel to share their ideas at any time. They shouldn't have to wait for leaders to come and ask their opinion.

Naturally, it shouldn't just be the leader that has these conversations. Every leader and manager should be expected to have these types of real conversations with their teams.

Certainly, you can add some other communication mechanisms in here. For example, Gary Kelly, CEO of Southwest Airlines, sends out weekly videos keeping people informed of what's changing. Email or intranet newsletters may come in handy to standardize communication and to communicate the same details to lots of people. But these do not take the place of real conversations with real people.

One more note: Many companies are reluctant to share information, especially before it's all ready. Except for a few domains where there are security, regulatory, or legal concerns, that is not a good strategy. Trust your people. Tell them what you're thinking and that you're going through a phase for everyone to absorb the direction. Use the law of communication that Gordon Bethune followed when he took over Continental Airlines, as reported by John Maxwell in his book *The 17 Indisputable Laws of Teamwork*: unless it's dangerous or illegal to share, we share it.

Company-wide communications do not take the place of real conversations with real people.

19

STEP 3: DO

THE NEXT STEP is to begin actual work on the goals—your distinct destination. The upper levels plan, the lower levels execute. But that doesn't mean disengaging on your part.

There are two parts to "doing": the execution and the continued conversation.

The execution part is to turn your people loose and let them do what they do best: execute. They develop the project plans, designs, and actually get work done—they accomplish what is now the Current Goal of the organization.

The continued conversation part means that you keep on doing the same things you did in the absorb phase: You have real conversations with people, and you stay engaged. This is important for multiple reasons.

First, you can ask questions about how the actual work is progressing. This serves to test people's understanding. Do they understand what's most important? Does everyone have the same belief and clarity about the destination? Have you actually created that clear reference point? Do they know what work is important? Are there problems that you did not anticipate? Spoiler alert: There will be. Inevitably, you will discover that you need to clear up their misconceptions and your communication.

Second, this serves as a feedback mechanism. As people actually get their hands dirty with the work of execution, clarity tends to disappear. John Kotter, considered by many as the grandfather of change management and the author of *Leading*

Change and *A Sense of Urgency*, says that these conversations help them re-establish clarity and make better decisions.

Bottom line: It's not just execution. It's execution plus lots of conversation.

There is one problem that often rears its head in this step. It's like our cat, Peaches, who is easily distracted by what's in front of her. When she is playing with a ball but happens to see a fish in our fish tank, she immediately leaves the ball and darts to the fish tank. When we get into the daily chaos of operations, we're like that. We get easily distracted. We lose focus on the organization's Ambition and Current Goal. We lose track of our own team's Immediate Objective. We chase after everything else that is immediately in front of us. Even worse, we can easily direct our teams' work in a manner that contradicts what we've said is most important. Teams become confused and frustrated.

> It's not just execution.
> It's execution plus lots of conversation.

There are three rhythms that are necessary to prevent these distractions and contradictions from naturally occurring:

1. *Get out of the chaos.* Coming from the software world, I recommend daily ten-minute check-ins along with your weekly team meetings. You cannot maintain focus if you do not have a set, prescribed rhythm to get out of the everyday chaos.

2. *Manage from Team One Sheets.* Every leader, manager and team member should be carrying around their Team One Sheet and using that as the foundation of day-to-day work and decisions.

3. *Schedule accountability briefings.* Leaders must insist that their direct reports, who are leading and managing their own teams, brief them regularly on the status of their team's Immediate Objective.

None of this means that teams and managers don't work on existing business operations. Of course they do. That's why they exist. They engineer products, initiate marketing campaigns, serve customers, develop software, you name it. They have the normal business objectives and metrics. But you won't make any progress if all your teams do is conduct normal operations. They must execute on what is most important for their team: its Immediate Objective. Perhaps they manufacture products, but their team's Immediate Objective is to manufacture them with a specific reduction in waste. Perhaps they develop software, but their team's Immediate Objective is to deliver on time on x percent of projects. That's how you make progress, and the only way to do that is to live from what's most important.

20

STEP 4: ADJUST

ONE OF THE most difficult aspects of coaching basketball is adjusting to what the other team is doing during the chaos of a game. It's also one of the keys to success.

You also must be able to adjust to the unexpected. To recognize when the conditions and needs have changed. To navigate around the clouds that will inevitably form on the horizon.

That is really, really hard to do if it's just you or your leadership team operating in a vacuum or if you have one leader who has all of the answers and makes all the decisions or if you never step back from the daily chaos. That is why this process is so important. By following the process, you will know what is going on so that you can adjust, understand and receive feedback on how to adjust, and be warned well before it hits you in the face.

Once you have identified a necessary adjustment, go back to Step 1 and create the adjustment with your leadership team. Then give people an opportunity to absorb it. That process may be quick depending on the scope of the adjustment, but you must still follow the process.

Now that your teams have a clear reference point to continuously refer back to and evaluate, they can work faster together to achieve it. As each team achieves their Immediate Objective, the team creates a new objective to continue to support the organization's Current Goal. As the organization together achieves its

Current Goal, senior leadership decides what the new Current Goal is for the organization, all with the intention of fulfilling the organization's Ultimate Ambition.

Before you know it, you'll have made significant progress—much faster and more meaningfully than when you were trying to achieve an equally important list of strategic priorities.

SUMMARY OF KEY POINTS

When your teams and departments are confused or have even the slightest level of ambiguity, they make up their own reference point based on their own interpretation of what's important. That makes it much more difficult for them to work together at lower levels, as you need them to do.

The basis of a clear reference point are three distinct organizational bearings so that every team can be assured that they are navigating to the same destination.

The three organizational bearings are:

1. The Ultimate Ambition of the organization
2. The Current Goal of the organization
3. The Immediate Objective of each team

The Team One Sheet is an important tool to embed the bearings into your daily operations.

The four steps to simplify your destination are:

1. Create: Create the three bearings with the entire leadership team; don't create it in a vacuum.
2. Absorb: Allow time for people to absorb, give input, and create their own team's Immediate Objective.
3. Do: Execute while continuing the conversation.
4. Adjust: Adjust as necessary.

Visit TheHippoSolution.com/bookresources for assessments, downloads, and additional resources.

IMMEDIATE ACTION STEPS

Take one of these quick action steps to take immediate action:

- <u>Visit the book resource page to assess this variable for your organization.</u>
- <u>Read *The Advantage* by Patrick Lencioni with your leadership team.</u>
  Lencioni's book provides an excellent overall model for organizational health, including the six questions to create the first organization bearing.
- <u>Read *The 4 Disciplines of Execution* with your leadership team.</u>
- <u>Schedule a strategic leadership team retreat right now—get it on the calendar.</u>
  Visit the book resource page for resources. Contact me for help to make it practical and productive.
- <u>Create a thematic goal.</u>
  Download the instructions from the book resource page to create a thematic goal, a.k.a. a Current Goal, leveraging Patrick Lencioni's model.
- <u>Write out every decision.</u>
  Before leaving your next meeting, write out the decisions that were made and ask for commitment to the decision, even if some did not initially agree with it. This ensures there are no differing perceptions of the decision that was made. Include action items and who owns each action item.

- <u>Share the most important goal with everyone.</u>
Create a single-page or business card-size document with the leadership team's three organizational bearings. Go share it with five people.

- <u>Conduct a knowledge flow session.</u>
Meet with a small group of people. Share the three organizational bearings. Then ask what's right, what's missing, and what's wrong with the leadership team's thinking.

- <u>Have a date night.</u>
Go out and have an informal conversation with a team or group. Share information, ask lots of questions, and just talk about change, the business, and life, similar to Tim Cook's "date nights."

- <u>Send a weekly video.</u>
Create a video and send that out to everyone to provide high-level information and answer questions regarding the organization's destination. This should not supplement real conversations.

Part 2
Restore Individuals

"A few hippos will often stay behind
to protect a young hippo calf from threats,
such as crocodiles and hyenas,
while the other hippos graze."
—San Francisco Zoo

$$\text{The Destination} \ \times \ \frac{\textbf{INDIVIDUALS} \times \text{Teams} \times \text{Gaps}}{\textbf{Organizational Constraints}}$$

21

THE STONES UNDER RUSHING WATER

THIS LAST SUMMER, our family took up kayaking on some of the rivers here in Middle Tennessee. Our first excursion was a three-hour affair down the Duck River. We thoroughly enjoyed easy paddling, stopping on sandbars, and seeing wildlife. It was enough to entice me to purchase two of our own kayaks and a car rack to transport them.

The next time we went kayaking with our own kayaks, we enjoyed a similar experience, although I noticed that the water level was a little lower on the smallish river.

The third time was a sunny weekend afternoon. After my daughter and I carried our kayaks down the stairs to the river—which was more like a large creek, really—we pushed off, happy to be on the water yet again. Once again, I noticed the water level was even lower this time. We hadn't had any rain lately, and I wondered if we would get stuck.

Sure enough, we hadn't traveled thirty feet before we reached an area of the river where the river narrowed and the water rushed over stones that were barely beneath the surface. As we shot through the narrow gap, our kayaks got stuck on the stones. We just sat there as the water rushed around us. We tried scooting on our bottoms. We tried pushing off the stones with our paddles. We were stuck.

Finally, we got out of our kayaks and pulled them to deeper water where we could continue our journey... until a couple hundred feet down the river where we got stuck again.

We want our teams to work together. We want our teams to be cohesive and high-functioning. But our teams are made of individuals. When individuals are not high-functioning, our teams can't be cohesive and high-functioning. When our teams are not cohesive and high-functioning, they can't work together with other teams to achieve what is most important for the organization.

Many individual leaders, managers, and team members are not high-functioning because they are getting stuck. Instead of physical stones, individuals in our workplace are getting stuck on the stones of stress, anxiety, fatigue, and burnout.

These "stones" have always been there—when has there not been workplace stress? The reason this is especially relevant now is that the "stones" have been accumulating while the water level has been lowering.

When individuals are not high-functioning, our teams can't be cohesive and high-functioning. When our teams are not cohesive and high-functioning, they can't work together with other teams to achieve what is most important for the organization.

We must address the stones under the rushing water.

My goal is very simple: to create a heightened awareness of the state of the individuals in your organization, to produce a realization of its effect on teams working together, and to provide a few simple, quick, easy actions for leaders to mitigate the effects.

22

THE STATE OF INDIVIDUALS AND ITS EFFECT

ACCORDING TO THE American Institute of Stress, ninety-four percent of U.S. workers report experiencing stress in the workplace while sixty-three percent of U.S. workers are ready to quit their jobs because of stress.

Deloitte reports that seventy-seven percent of workers have experienced burnout at their current job. A Gallup survey found that sixty-seven percent of full-time employees experience burnout very often, always, or sometimes.

The *Harvard Business Review* refers to this as the "global epidemic of stress and burnout."

This isn't your grandparents' stress. It's a convergence of factors that has created compounding stress.

There are workplace factors: an almost constant pressure to perform; being pressed to meet high, sometimes unrealistic, performance standards; expectations that have risen without thought or care for the resulting stress; the need to perform the job of two or more people; everything seems important; change that no longer ends; business conditions that are changing constantly.

There are economic factors: personal debt loads, the expense of getting kids through life, taking care of elderly parents, living paycheck to paycheck, lack of savings, job security that no longer exists.

The Harvard Business Review refers to this as the "global epidemic of stress and burnout."

There are technological factors: the speed of information means more information to process, more decisions in which to be involved, and the blurring of work and personal life. In addition, the speed of information also means involving more decision-makers, adding complexity to getting things done.

There are cultural factors: People are asking questions about racism, justice, and unrest. What does this mean? What is my part in this? How does it affect me? The divide of political beliefs and opinions is off the charts, personal issues such as broken relationships are common, and we want to understand our purpose and have meaning, but society is not providing adequate answers.

This convergence of factors has created a high level of stress that has, is, or will affect almost every leader, manager, and team member in your workplace.

To be fair, there are different types of stress, some of which may actually enhance team performance, such as a team challenge that requires new ways of thinking and team collaboration to achieve. What we are talking about here is individual, compounding stress—some call it quantitative stress—an ever-increasing stress load from multiple sources.

The sources of compounding stress are the stones under rushing water.

At the same time, the water level is low. Individuals no longer have the passion, purpose, and engagement to cover up the stones. Deloitte found that only 13.9 percent have the level of passion to take on new challenges and connect with others. *Harvard Business Review* reports almost identical results: only thirteen percent of U.S. workers "exhibited the type of passion to improve in their profession."

The stones are numerous, and the water level is low.

What does this have to do with teams working together? When individuals experience stress, it creates distraction, a narrowing focus, and de-identification. As a result, team performance suffers.

Multiple studies have shown this correlation between stress and a negative impact on teams, including the tendency to narrow our focus, retreat into territorial thinking, and de-identify from the team. De-identifying with our own team and narrowing our focus is the opposite of what we need: We need for team members to establish a strong identity with their own teams and broaden their focus to work and collaborate with other teams.

How can we possibly get teams to work together if individual leaders and team members are focusing inward and pulling away from others?

23
CONDUCT A CLEARING TURN

BEFORE YOU START any practice maneuver when training for a pilot's license, you always conduct a clearing turn to make sure the area is clear of other airplanes. You turn ninety degrees in one direction, looking out the windows for other airplanes, then turn ninety degrees in the other direction. Once you've confirmed the area is clear, you start your maneuver.

Before we launch initiatives or implement stronger teamwork practices to get teams to work together, we need to perform a "clearing turn." A clearing turn means taking simple actions to mitigate the effects of stress, burnout, and lack of passion that so many are experiencing.

Sara Potecha, a leadership expert, speaker, and author, writes about "recovering while you work." She talks about how the little, simple habits make a big difference—not the big sweeping changes.

I am not asking for you to play the role of a therapist or launch some huge cultural initiative. I am asking you to build into your rhythm a few quick, simple actions that will make a difference in your individuals, because the "stones" can no longer be ignored. They are affecting team performance.

Naturally, we can't just start with actions. We can't simply go through the motions. We need to embrace *restoring others* as a leadership calling. As leaders, as managers, it's part of who we are. We're not just there to perform. We're not just there to get others to perform. We're also there to restore—to make other's lives better.

It's our responsibility, our calling, as leaders to create healthy individuals on our teams and in our organizations.

In the Bible, the book of Joel talks about "restoring the years that the locusts have eaten." You are in a unique position to help your individual team members restore what has been taken away by stress, burnout, never-ending change, and difficult situations.

That seems like a tall order, but all it takes is 5-3-1.

It's our responsibility as leaders to create healthy individuals on our teams and in our organizations.

24
THE 5-3-1 MODEL

WHEN I WORK with senior leaders and managers, I recommend leveraging the 5-3-1 model in their daily and weekly rhythms:

- 5 Actions
- 3 Goals
- 1 Motive

5 Actions

We start with actions because I want you to see how easy it is to restore others. The 5 in the 5-3-1 model refers to five actions, any of which you can take right now—today. The five actions, represented by the acrostic iStop, are:

1. Inject fun.
2. Spend one-on-one time.
3. Take care of yourself.
4. Openly talk about stress, anxiety, and mental wellness.
5. Provide growth opportunities.

Action #1: Inject fun

Find something to do that's out of the ordinary. Go have fun. Inject humor and laughter into your meetings. Play. It doesn't have to be a big team-building experience. Conduct a scavenger hunt or go bowling. Do something different. Even if you are operating remotely, inject a fun game or competition into a meeting such as playing Kahoot! or conducting a Zoom scavenger hunt. There are many ways to have a little fun and laughter.

Action #2: Spend one-on-one time

Schedule one-on-one time with each of your direct reports. Encourage them to spend one-on-one time with their own direct reports. Don't even have an agenda. Talk about whatever is on their mind—work items and life issues. What's going on in their lives? What's going on in their minds? It's a time to build connection and support. Get to know your people as individuals so you'll know how to help them contribute to a healthy workplace. Ask good questions. For example, "What do you mean by...?" or "What makes you say that?" or "What is causing you to be anxious?" or "What's important to you about...?" Ask passion questions such as, "What pursuits would inspire and give you meaning?" or "What impact would you like to make on others?"

Action #3: Take care of yourself

I love a good Western—book or movie, it doesn't matter. One of my favorite Western writers is Louis L'Amour. I can devour one of his novels in one sitting even though I already know the plot: the rugged individualist pursuing a goal while minding his own business when he comes across a nefarious character that is inflicting some sort of injustice on the people that the rugged individualist cares about. The rugged individualist stands in the gap, fights through the inevitable adversity, and single-handedly inflicts justice on the nefarious character.

It's always a fun story... and a terrible example.

Yes, we need to be resilient and overcome adversity, but we also need to take time to take care of ourselves—you could say to restore our own self. Otherwise, how can we help others?

When I spoke to a group of leaders at a local hospital, Sharon Ball, a mental wellness professional and trauma expert, also taught one of the sessions, during which she recommended thinking about self-care in three categories: physical, emotional, and social.

Physical: What is one activity that you can start right now—perhaps one that you stopped doing in the past? These are simple actions: taking a walk during lunch, getting half an hour more sleep, drinking more water, or practicing intentional breathing.

Emotional: We spend so much time taking in information, but we can't process it that quickly. Take five to ten minutes each day in solitude—which is different than isolation—to simply reflect.

Social: Who do you need to reach out to? Where is your social support lacking? Call, text, or message someone right now to enhance your social support.

All of these ideas are really simple and take minutes—seconds, even—to implement.

Action #4: Openly talk about stress, anxiety, and mental wellness

There has been a stigma around talking about anything related to stress, anxiety, burnout, mental wellness, and similar topics. Only fourteen percent of people are comfortable speaking with their manager about stress. Change that dynamic in your team and organization. Open up a meeting by talking about a related article. Watch a YouTube video on mental wellness or stress. Invite an expert in to conduct a webinar or talk. Make it easier to talk about these topics by talking about them.

Action #5: Provide growth opportunities

Help your team members discover their strengths. Take an assessment, such as the Strengths Deployment Inventory, the VIA Character Strengths Survey, or Patrick Lencioni's Working Genius Assessment. Intentionally give them opportunities to use their strengths and to develop new skills. How can you bring out the best in them?

None of these five actions are difficult or time-consuming. Many can be done in minutes. Pick one and do it—today.

3 Goals

The five actions roll up into three overall goals that we need to adopt:

1. Meet our team members' higher-level needs
2. Create an environment of fun and enjoyment
3. Find ways to bring out the best in your team members

Goal #1: Meet our team members' higher-level needs

Chris Conley, in his book *Peak*, talks about leveraging Maslow's hierarchy of needs to meet the *higher* needs of your individual leaders, managers, and team members. His "transformation pyramid" provides the model: survival needs (receiving adequate compensation), success needs (being recognized), and transformation needs (creating a sense of meaning). Yes, make sure your team members are properly compensated, but don't stop there. Provide in-person personal praise, ask questions to understand their personal calling, and tie their calling into their work.

Goal #2: Add enjoyment to the lives of your team members

Anything can be fun if you are intentional about creating a fun environment. Go out of the way to do something different and have a little fun. Be enthusiastic—it's contagious. Add enjoyment to the lives of your people.

Goal #3: Find ways to bring out the best in your team members

Jon Gordon, in his book *The Energy Bus*, writes specifically about bringing out the best in others—a natural result of loving them. He talks about helping our team members identify their strengths and providing opportunities for them.

1 Motive

Our motive drives everything: our behaviors, our goals, our actions, our decisions. You can't restore individuals if you don't have the right motive.

If you take on the calling of restoring your people, the one motive is to serve others. That's it. It's not to achieve, to be approved, to be comfortable, to be loved, to perform, to get something. It's to serve others.

Certainly, we are called upon to perform, and we must do so. But we do that with the motive of serving others. This motive has been articulated in different ways by so many. For example, John Maxwell describes leadership itself as "adding value to people." In his book *The Motive*, Patrick Lencioni encourages a responsibility-based leadership motive. In the Bible, Jesus preaches about serving others.

Serving others is gratifying, satisfying, and fuel for your soul. Serving ourselves is empty, devoid of meaning, and exhausting. Not only that, but you get better performance from people when your true heart's motive is to serve them.

It doesn't take much to raise the water level and help your individual leaders, managers, and team members get unstuck so that the power of teams is unleashed. It just takes intentionality.

Would you like a bonus action?

Lenora Billings-Harris, a well-known speaker and author on diversity, recently spoke about how our most critical need is actually *belonging*. We want to feel that we belong to something, which means that creating a strong context of teams is actually another action to restore individuals.

Which brings us to our next variable.

SUMMARY OF KEY POINTS

When individuals are not high-functioning, our teams can't be cohesive and high-functioning. When our teams are not cohesive and high-functioning, they can't work together with other teams to achieve what is most important for the organization.

Individual leaders, managers, and team members are experiencing a convergence of workplace, economic, technological, and cultural factors leading to compounding, or quantitative, stress, anxiety, burnout, and fatigue. Individuals are also experiencing a lack of passion, purpose, and engagement that would ordinarily compensate.

The 5-3-1 model provides an everyday framework to help individuals.

- 5 Actions: inject fun; spend one-on-one time; take care of yourself; openly talk about stress, anxiety, and mental wellness; provide opportunities.
- 3 Goals: meet your team members' higher-level needs, add enjoyment to their lives, find ways to bring out the best in your team members.
- 1 Motive: serve others.

Visit TheHippoSolution.com/bookresources for assessments, downloads, and additional resources.

IMMEDIATE ACTION STEPS

Take one of these quick action steps to take immediate action:

- <u>Visit the book resource page to assess this variable for your organization.</u>
- <u>Read *Peak* by Chris Conley with your leadership team.</u>
  Conley's book provides a great model for meeting the higher-level needs of your individuals.
- <u>Read *The Motive* by Patrick Lencioni with your leadership team.</u>
  Begin a discussion about the motive that is driving the leadership brand and the behaviors of each of your senior leaders.
- <u>Do something fun in your next meeting.</u>
  Play Kahoot, conduct a Zoom scavenger hunt, or Google ideas for fun or icebreakers in meetings.
- <u>Take a Working Genius assessment with your leadership team.</u>
  Dig into the natural working genius of everyone on your team. Visit the book resource page for information on how to take the assessment.
- <u>Take a walk during lunch.</u>
- <u>Spend five minutes tonight to reflect on something you learned today.</u>
- <u>Reach out to a friend who you have not reached out to in some time.</u>
- <u>Watch a YouTube video about workplace stress and anxiety during your next meeting.</u>

Part 3
Strengthen Teams

"Hippos are social, living in a group of ten
to thirty animals called a herd."
—San Diego Zoo

$$\text{The Destination} \times \frac{\text{Individuals} \times \textbf{TEAMS} \times \text{Gaps}}{\text{Organizational Constraints}}$$

25

AROUND THE ISLAND

NESTLED IN THE Adirondack mountains of northeastern New York is an island in the middle of a beautiful lake. This lake is the setting for a youth summer camp. This lake was also the setting for one of my more epic life achievements.

In the middle of the week was the infamous canoe race around the island. Our cabin was chosen as one of the competitors, and I was somehow chosen to be on the canoe team for our cabin. By "somehow," I mean that I managed to manipulate my way onto the canoe team because I love paddling canoes.

As I put on my life jacket and picked up my oar, I sized up the three other boats in the race. First boat, no problem. Second boat, no threat. Neither of the rowers in these boats looked like they had the strength or the skills to be a serious threat. The third boat, on the other hand, was different: There sat two athletic-looking boys, both of whom appeared stronger, older, and more athletic-looking than my canoe mate and me. I decided to call them Bert and Ernie. As we walked past them on the way to our canoe, I heard no small amount of boasting. They knew who was going to win. Well, game on.

The race started off as one might expect. The "favorites" took the lead with a torrid pace while we gradually pulled away from the other two canoes.

As we reached the first turn, Bert and Ernie were starting to wear out, and they were no longer in the shelter of the harbor. They now had to row with the waves and execute the turns necessary to navigate around the island. Working together to navigate the canoe became much more important with the new complexities of the open lake.

We slowly gained on them, easily navigating the first turn. While we didn't have the same level of strength, age, or athletic prowess, we had some pretty good teamwork and were building a nice rhythm together. Two strokes on one side, switch, two strokes on the other side, switch, two strokes on... Never over-exerting, always steady.

By the time we reached the second turn, about a quarter of the way around the island, we had caught up to them, much to their surprise—and my delight. Their response was to paddle harder. While it gave them an initial advantage, it was to no avail because they couldn't keep up that level of effort, and our team synergy was just too good.

We pulled away and never looked back.

It wasn't strength or individual skills. It was working together as a cohesive team. It was teamwork that won the day.

As we were approaching the dock at the very end of the race, far ahead of Bert and Ernie, I looked back. They had given up, deliberately flipping their canoe in order to take a swim in the lake.

We had won!

But it wasn't strength or individual skills. It was working together as a cohesive team. It was *teamwork* that won the day.

As it is in our organizations.

However, teamwork isn't winning the day in our organizations so much these days. It's time for that to change.

26

WHY TEAMWORK MATTERS MORE THAN EVER

HOW WE WORK is and has been changing. Deloitte reported that organizations are shifting from a traditional hierarchy to a network of teams approach and a shared team structure.

Wiley reports that teams are "becoming more complex, more fluid, and more remote." Seventy-six percent of people report being on two or more teams—five or more teams if you are a director or executive. Seventy-three percent of people report being on two or more <u>types</u> of teams, such as project-based, departmental, or matrix teams. Many teams are mixed with contractors and form quickly, do work, and "disassemble."

Deloitte further reported on research that the leadership function is shifting to a collaborative function, with a shifting focus on a leader's ability to work more collaboratively across functions and enhance team performance.

Success requires a highly functioning team of highly functioning teams if you want your organization to work together, operate at a high level, execute quickly, and change more easily.

There is a gradual recognition at the highest levels that the world has become too complex for a single authoritarian leader who makes all the decisions and who knows everything.

Success requires a highly functioning *team* of highly functioning *teams* if you want your organization to work together, operate at a high level, execute quickly, and change more easily.

How could we possibly expect teams to work well with other teams if they aren't functioning at a high level themselves?

Several domains have already dedicated resources to developing high-functioning teams, recognizing their importance. Commercial airlines have long poured resources into "crew resource management," essentially cockpit teamwork training, correctly identifying the lack of working together as a contributor to airline crashes and mishaps in past decades. The military emphasizes high-functioning units in their officer training—my son's ROTC training being just one example. Healthcare has been emphasizing teamwork more and more to prevent clinical mistakes.

What would have happened had I approached Patrick Air Force Base as a team instead of operating as a lone pilot? Would I have still landed at the wrong airport? Almost certainly not.

It's time for all of us to take teamwork seriously.

27

THE STATE OF TEAMS

THERE IS A large gap between the perceived and actual effectiveness of individual teams.

According to the State of Teams report published by Wiley, while engaging with teams takes over sixty percent of an employee's time, four in five people report that their team members are typically not willing to acknowledge their weaknesses, highlighting a pervasive lack of vulnerability-based trust. Three in five say that team members refuse to take personal responsibility. Seventy-five percent have been in a toxic team environment. Eighty-eight percent report being on teams where a lack of cohesion hurt their team's productivity. Nine in ten people say their organizational culture would improve if people were more effective teammates.

The result of mediocre teamwork in the organization is not unlike a football team where the offensive line is not working as a cohesive unit or an orchestra where the percussion section is not playing together. The dysfunction of that one unit affects the entire orchestra. That's the kind of impact on the organization when individual teams are not high-functioning and cohesive.

28
THE SIX REASONS

BEFORE WE PRESCRIBE a solution, it is necessary to recognize and acknowledge why individual teams are not high-functioning. Otherwise, we don't know what should be different and why. There are six common reasons for mediocre teamwork.

Reason #1: Teamwork is hard, sometimes unrewarding work.

It's not easy creating a high-functioning, cohesive team. While the rewards are tremendous, it takes work. It takes intentionality. It sometimes takes difficult conversations.

The temptation as a leader is to focus on the busy-ness—on the work itself. It's easier that way. Why add one more thing to my plate? Why confront that poor behavior? Why have that difficult conversation? Why spend time on teamwork—that may even reflect poorly on me to some extent?

The temptation as a team member is to focus on my tasks instead of on the team. I'm busy enough as it is—why spend time on teamwork? Why work with someone who is slowing me down? Why work on teamwork when I'll probably end up doing someone else's work? Or giving credit to the team for my work? If I succeed at a task, I get the credit. If we succeed as a team, we share the credit.

Reason #2: We focus on individuals over teams.

The temptation when coaching a sport like basketball is to focus on your stars—how to get them the ball and enable them to score—at the expense of the other players. It's the same with your "shining stars" at work. Because they do so much and want to do more, it's so easy to lean on "shining stars," develop them, give them more responsibility, call them "emerging leaders," and rely on them to carry the day at the expense of teamwork. Work needs to get done, and it's awfully hard not to lean on your best players.

Because they do so much and want to do more, it's so easy to lean on "shining stars," develop them, give them more responsibility, call them "emerging leaders," and rely on them to carry the day at the expense of teamwork.

This is evidenced in many leadership development and incentive programs—those programs naturally focus on individuals and individual performance over teams and team performance.

Reason #3: We leverage contradictory old and new thinking.

While respected firms like Deloitte are reporting how the workplace has and is turning into a world of teams, there is natural tension with previous structures and thinking. We still tend to be structured hierarchically, which creates competing agendas. There's nothing wrong with hierarchical structures—we need organization—but we still deal with strong hierarchical *thinking*. Many leaders still have the view that they should be the one who understands everything and thus be the one to make all the decisions. In many ways, we still lead with a hybrid of old and new thinking.

Reason #4: We misunderstand what it means to be a highly functioning team.

When I was a project manager at a technology company, we had a good team of project managers that got along, supported each other, held each other accountable, and were committed to the same goals. It was the same for the cross-functional team I led—or so I thought at the time.

One of the teams I had been working with had worked hard for several weeks on an important software release, which included specific features that our young company desperately needed in order to generate more revenue and attract new customers.

Three days before the release date, our team ran into a problem. There were a couple of critical software defects that would prevent customers from using the new functionality. A fix would be risky. We had to release simultaneously with two other teams—there was shared code between the three teams—and we didn't have time to conduct proper testing. The decision was made to release the software as is with the defects and without the fix. Customers and revenue would have to wait.

End of story, right? Not so fast.

On the surface, the problem was just a mistake that someone made, but with the benefit of more experience, knowledge, and insight, there were team-work issues at play. Information did not flow freely between different elements of the team, such as between developers and product managers. There were side conversations. There was not a healthy, spirited debate amongst the team to determine the best course of action. Two groups had a subtle lack of trust between each other. It wasn't overt, it didn't come out in meetings, but it was there, as I learned later. All of these affected both the ability to catch the problem earlier and to properly debate the best decision in the moment.

Teams appear to be a good team on the surface—they get along and get work done—but getting along and getting work done is not the same as being a high-functioning team. There is a distinct difference.

This is what happens so often in organizations. Teams *appear* to be a good team on the surface—they get along and get work done—but getting along and getting work done is not the same as being a high-functioning team. There is a distinct difference. I did not understand the difference at the time.

Despite my schooling and project management training, I had very little knowledge of what a high-functioning team looked like. As long as we were getting along and getting work done, I figured we were a good team and I was a good leader. But high-functioning, highly cohesive teams go far beyond this.

According to Patrick Lencioni in his highly acclaimed book, *The Five Dysfunctions of a Team*, considered by many the standard of what it means to be a cohesive team, high-functioning teams have strong vulnerability-based trust, they have passionate debates around ideas, they commit to decisions, they hold each other accountable, and they don't get distracted by what's not important.

Most teams stick with what's comfortable, unwilling to have the tough conversations, the spirited debate, or to hold each other accountable. As a result, many teams consider themselves "good teams" but are sitting on a teamwork issue that is holding back their performance. Becoming a great, high-functioning, cohesive team is hard work but yields a significant increase in performance—both the performance of the individual team and the performance of multiple teams as they work more closely together.

Reason #5: We don't have a consistent framework and language to talk about teams and how we work together.

We all come from different backgrounds with different team experiences and different assumptions on what it means to be a good team. Most teams don't have a consistent framework and common organizational language around the behaviors that make up a high-functioning team. This results in different teams in the same or different departments having a different standard for teamwork based on the leader's knowledge, opinion, and sometimes, their whim.

Reason #6: The leadership team isn't cohesive.

Many leadership teams don't take this seriously enough to work on it themselves. As a result, the leadership team is not high-functioning and cohesive. I don't mean they don't get along or that they always have major issues. I mean that they are not operating at nearly the level needed to be considered high-functioning and highly cohesive. The result is that no other team will take it seriously either.

That is why one of the most productive, impactful ways I help organizations is to work with their executive leadership teams to first become highly functioning and cohesive.

———————————

Now, how do we strengthen teams?

> Is your team high-functioning and cohesive? Visit the book resource page to find out by taking a team assessment.

29
THE FOUR STEPS

DURING THE BEGINNING of every youth soccer season I coached, in the first game, the same behavior would emerge. A girl would receive the ball. What came next was predictable: She would put her head down, look at the ball, attempt to dribble past the defender, then the next defender, and literally try to dribble through the entire opposing team. By herself. Of course, even if she was a superstar, the ball would inevitably be taken away from her by someone on the opposing team.

I would coach my heart out from the sideline. "Pass the ball!" "Keep your head up!" "Look for your teammate!" But it didn't do any good.

The reality is that she was just following what came naturally. "I have the ball, my job is to go score." And she went about doing her job.

In the very early years of my coaching, I would lament my player's lack of teamwork. That was both simplistic and wrong.

The issue was not that she wouldn't pass the ball or work with her teammates. The issue had nothing to do with her. The issue was me. The issue was how I was coaching. I didn't have a system for teaching teamwork. There wasn't a context of teamwork that had been drilled in. And so she, along with her teammates, were just doing what came naturally: their jobs.

I had to create a system to develop the kind of teamwork we needed to succeed. I had to drill teamwork from the very first practice to the very last one. **"Pass the ball" had to become a mantra.**

It's the same thing in your organization. It's not enough to stand on the sidelines and call out for people to work together. You need a system to "drill" teamwork and create the context of desired behaviors around every team, just like on my soccer teams.

There are four key steps to create and instill a system of teamwork:

Step #1: Adopt a Teamwork Framework: The framework defines the specific language and behaviors that you want your teams to adopt.

It's not enough to stand on the sidelines and call out for people to work together. You need a system to "drill" teamwork and create the context of desired behaviors around every team.

Step #2: Build a Cohesive Leadership Team: When the leadership team adopts the behaviors and becomes cohesive, it has a positive effect on the entire organization while setting the example on how teams should function.

Step #3: Drill Teamwork Behaviors into Every Team: Teams need to become cohesive by leveraging cost-effective methods of drilling teamwork into every single team.

Step #4: Resolve the Two Common Teamwork Issues: You must address two common but often overlooked teamwork issues that prevent cohesive teams.

30
STEP #1: ADOPT A TEAMWORK FRAMEWORK

THE FIRST STEP is to adopt a common framework and language around teamwork that every team can leverage.

When I work with leadership and other teams in organizations, I typically leverage the model from Patrick Lencioni's book *The Five Dysfunctions of a Team*. His book has sold over three million copies, has helped countless teams become cohesive, and has related assessments easily accessible. Lencioni's model is the very definition of what it means to be a high-functioning, highly cohesive team. All you have to do is read the book or go to the book resource page for links and materials to learn about the model.

I also recommend Lencioni's Humble, Hungry, and Smart model from his book, *The Ideal Team Player*. Together, these two models provide both the concrete behaviors that should be present when a team is working together and the virtues of what makes a good team member.

If you would like to create your own teamwork framework for how teams operate based on your own experience, go for it. However, I suggest that you simply choose one that has already been developed. It's both easier and time-tested. However, it's not enough to simply *choose* a teamwork framework. You need to embed it. Develop a chart with the expected team behaviors that comes directly from the framework. Review them at every team meeting at every level throughout the organization.

This all works to establish your culture as an organization and your brand as a leader.

Many organizations embrace this type of approach. For example, Disney uses the seven guest service guidelines to establish the expected behaviors of cast members with guests. Alan Mulally created a "One Ford" card. On the back were employees' expected behaviors.

Visit the book resource page for information on specific resources to read about and leverage as your framework.

31
STEP #2: BUILD A COHESIVE LEADERSHIP TEAM

IF YOUR LEADERSHIP team is not cohesive and high-functioning, you cannot have an organization filled with cohesive, high-functioning teams. Too many executives look at working on teamwork as something for "the other teams" in the organization.

This is unfortunate because making your executive leadership team more cohesive and high-functioning is the single most impactful action you can take to get your entire organization to work together in a more cohesive and high-functioning manner.

It has *that* level of impact.

This is not a one-time event. You don't just develop your leadership team once. You establish a rhythm—a system—to build an executive leadership team that is continuously pushing itself to be more and more high-functioning and cohesive. This is not a training session or a retreat. It is a rhythm—a way of operating.

> *If your leadership team is not cohesive and high-functioning, you cannot have an organization filled with cohesive, high-functioning teams.*

The rhythm needs to include the following elements:

1. Regular team assessments and debriefs

There is no substitute for seeing how the team is actually doing in black and white (or green, yellow, red). Too often, there is a facade that all is well, when in reality, there are issues holding the team back. A team assessment is a natural, non-threatening way to bring those issues to light in a productive conversation, coupled with a dialogue around how the team behaves, how that affects the team's performance, and how the team can improve. Sometimes, there are behaviors that need to be addressed in order for the team to move forward. Other times, the team just needs an honest conversation about what it is doing well and which areas of focus will best move it forward. Great teams have these types of conversations. Mediocre and average teams don't.

Your leadership team cannot know how to become more cohesive and high-functioning if it does not both assess itself and have the conversations to discover on which areas it needs to work. This should be done regularly—at least every six months—to measure progress and know what to work on next. Naturally, my favorite assessment is based on Patrick Lencioni's *The Five Dysfunctions of a Team* model. It only takes ten to fifteen minutes to complete the assessment. Visit the book resource page for resources and to conduct an assessment for your team.

2. Regular retreats

Your leadership team must regularly take time for the team to step back from the chaos. The leadership team is the team that has the most significant impact on the direction, health, and alignment of the entire organization. It is worth spending a couple of days to focus on getting things right.

It is not unusual for leadership teams to take retreats, but they are often focused on developing business strategy or making concrete plans. They also need to be focused on developing the leadership team itself. These are not training sessions or boring lectures but strategic working sessions—it's a time to get work done and answer tough questions together.

When I facilitate a retreat for executive leadership teams, the agenda often includes a mix of key components including:

- A team assessment and debrief
- Making meetings much more productive and impactful

- A new leader assimilation process (when there is a new leader)
- Determining the Current Goal for the organization
- Answering Patrick Lencioni's six questions for organizational clarity
- Establishing rhythms to both maintain focus on what's most important and to effectively communicate well with the rest of the organization

---

Darren Harris is the CEO of the Bone and Joint Institute in Franklin, Tennessee. According to Harris, "Our leadership team has to be constantly learning and nimble because healthcare changes quickly. It's a challenge to make sure that we are all aligned and sharing that with the rest of the organization." Harris takes his leadership team off-site on a leadership retreat twice a year, once in December and once in June, because of how important it is for him to collaborate with the team, for the team to formulate and own collective goals and solutions, and for the team to make good decisions. It's important that every leader is aligned and knows their exact responsibilities.

Oftentimes, the temptation is to stay in the whirlwind of everyday operations and not take the time to get that collaboration and clean commitment or to rely on a single leader to make all of the decisions. Both are mistakes that hurt performance, increase politics, and slow down the organization.

---

3. Team One Sheet

Leadership teams need Team One Sheets to ensure that they are executing and making decisions based on what they've determined to be their most important goal. The Team One

Sheet, covered in Part 1, should also include the specific focus area on which the team is working to become more cohesive coming out of the team assessment. For example, the team may have a focus of acknowledging weaknesses to one another in order to build vulnerability-based trust on the team. This needs to remain a focus.

32
THE 10-3-2-1 RHYTHM

10-3-2-1 IS A tool to help leadership teams establish a rhythm for building stronger teamwork, negating the tendency of teamwork being a short-term passing fad. The tool forces the team to continuously improve and lead the organization from a position of health—meaning minimal politics, clear direction, and cohesive teamwork.

The 10-3-2-1 rhythm is:

- 10 minutes every day for the team to review what's most important and other tactical matters for the day
- 3 retreats per year where the team gets away from the daily chaos to work on itself—alignment, cohesiveness, high functioning, direction
- 2 conversations per day by every member of the team with other people in the organization to communicate and clarify direction
- 1 current goal at all times

You can certainly customize the 10-3-2-1 rhythm for your team's needs. In fact, the magic is not so much in the specific behaviors so much as having a distinct rhythm to constantly work on cohesiveness and alignment. The advantage of this type of tool is that it keeps the team focused on building a high-functioning, cohesive team. The 10-3-2-1 rhythm should be included on your Team One Sheet.

One final note: This rhythm should be done by your executive leadership team, but it shouldn't stop there. It should also be done for all high-impact teams. If you are leading a department or a division, you need to implement the rhythm with the leadership team of that department or division. Any team that has a high level of impact on the organization needs to take the time and energy to be high-functioning and cohesive.

33

STEP #3: DRILL TEAMWORK BEHAVIORS INTO EVERY TEAM

WHILE IT IS critical for your executive leadership and other high-impact teams to be high-functioning and cohesive, it obviously shouldn't stop there. Every team in the organization needs to be high-functioning and cohesive. The level of execution and cohesiveness of those individual teams has a direct bearing on the level of execution and cohesiveness of the entire organization.

In addition, for the goal of this book, how can we expect teams to work together if they are not cohesive and high-functioning themselves?

However, it may be unrealistic from a cost and time perspective to implement the same level of effort for all of the other teams in the organization as you do for the executive leadership team. For one thing, there are probably a large number of teams both traditional and non-traditional, role-based and cross-functional. However, it's still important—too often, these "other teams" are not given the resources needed to become cohesive themselves unless there is a teamwork problem that has to be "fixed." If this is the case, you're missing out on a tremendous opportunity and leaving out a key variable for teams across the organization to work together.

The approach for the rest of the teams is five-fold: to establish teamwork behavior standards, teach them to your teams, expect teams to exhibit those behaviors, give leaders and managers exposure, and provide high-impact supporting resources. This is a reasonable, cost-effective approach to provide a strong context of teamwork throughout the entire organization.

Establish teamwork behavior standards

Set a clear standard for teamwork behaviors. This includes both the behaviors that teams should adopt as well as how individuals treat each other. This comes from the teamwork framework, such as Lencioni's model, as well as your expected behaviors of individuals.

Teach the teamwork behavior standards

Naturally, you need to teach the behavior standards to your team. There are multiple methods of teaching the standards. When I conduct training workshops or webinars, the purpose is often to teach the teamwork framework to teams and team leaders throughout the organization. You could conduct book studies of a book that articulates the teamwork model or watch a series of videos. It is especially effective when senior executives take the time to share teamwork standards with team leaders—it lends credibility and importance, even if this is just for a few minutes at the beginning of a workshop, webinar, or book study.

Expect teams to exhibit those behaviors

The teamwork behavioral standards are never broken—no exceptions. Alan Mulally called this "joyful accountability." Hold your teams accountable to the standard. Of course, this only works if your executive leadership team sets the example and believes in the power of teams working together cohesively.

I recommend that you employ a "three-for-one" approach. When I coach basketball and plan practices, I look for drills that accomplish two or three objectives at once, such as ball handling, layups, passing, and offensive plays. Embrace the same approach. Set up debrief sessions with your teams or team leaders to report not just on the status of initiatives but on areas of teamwork on which they are working, how those teamwork areas are coming along, and the team's Immediate Objective.

Give leaders and managers exposure to leading teams

When you coach a basketball team, you want to get as many practices in as you can before the first game. In reality, there are diminishing returns. Players have to play in games. They have to be exposed to game situations. That is where they—as well as coaches—really learn and improve.

Same thing with your leaders and managers. Josh Bersin, a leading researcher and adviser in enterprise learning and talent management, advocates for the benefits of *exposure* as a development method over traditional leadership development programs. Placing leaders and managers where they are exposed to different people, leadership, and team situations is placing them where they must learn and develop. Give them as much opportunity as possible to build the right behaviors to create highly functional teams.

Of course, many teams are matrix teams or cross-functional teams where there is not a hierarchical leader. It may be a program manager or a project manager with leadership responsibilities for the team but with no actual authority. The same principle and behaviors apply. Give those leaders exposure to leading teams and expect them to build in the organization's foundational teamwork behaviors. It's just as important in hybrid types of teams.

Provide high-impact supporting resources

While leaders and managers throughout the organization are leading and building their highly functional teams, they need consistent supporting resources. These resources should include a mix of the following elements:

- **Team assessments**: Teams should be able to take and debrief their own assessments—perhaps with an internal or external coach to guide them—and have a resulting specific area of focus to become more cohesive. Visit the book resource page for information on team assessments.

- **Mentors/coaches**: Mentors and coaches are the most impactful resource you can provide for your leaders and managers, according to Bersin, as they lead teams. Provide these resources to work through team issues and maintain accountability to team cohesiveness. Sometimes, you may need to start with external mentors/coaches until you establish internal expertise.

- **Immediate Objective of the Team**: As we covered earlier, every single team must be expected to create their own Immediate Objective that supports the organization's Current Goal. Insist that they always have one and that it is relevant. Having this goal supports the team's efforts to develop high-functioning teamwork.

- **Meeting resources**: So many meetings are wasted time and energy, but when meetings become great, it changes everything. Teams need resources to help them have great, highly effective meetings because this is where much of the team's work together is done.

- **External resource**: When I work with organizations long-term, having an external resource ends up being valuable for team leaders—they can call, and we can walk through all sorts of team situations together without any fear of retribution or feeling foolish. Consider setting up a similar resource for your teams.

- **Strategic mega-sessions**: A mega-session takes multiple teams and walks them through a team assessment and debrief at the same time, either in the same room or in the same Zoom meeting with breakouts. When I conduct training workshops, I find that this is a great way to teach the teamwork framework, conduct assessments, and impact multiple teams at once without the cost of a dedicated facilitator/expert for each individual team.

- **Books**: Give your teams books for them to learn the framework, such as Patrick Lencioni's *The Five Dysfunctions of a Team*. Suggestion: Give them the manga edition to make it more likely they will read it.

- **Online resources**: It's not very difficult to create a set of online resources, such as links to webinars, videos and articles, for teams to take advantage of. They don't have to be created internally. There are many resources out there. Visit the book resource page for ideas.

- **Team One Sheets**: Just like your executive leadership team needs a Team One Sheet, every team in your organization needs one too. Make templates available to every team and expect them to use it. Team One Sheets promote teamwork.

- **"Teamwork Quips"**: One of my clients had a daily "Safety Quip" that was read at every meeting. It was a brief bit about promoting workplace safety. Employ a daily or weekly "Teamwork Quip," and have teams read it at every meeting.

If you feel that you do not have the bandwidth to put in place high-quality supporting resources, visit the book resource page for ideas and templates and to learn about our company's program to provide resources for you.

Visit the book resource page for related resources to provide for your teams.

34
STEP #4: RESOLVE THESE TWO COMMON TEAMWORK ISSUES

THERE ARE TWO common issues that are difficult yet important to resolve if you want to implement strong teamwork. Otherwise, they hold back your teams from working together, both within an individual team and across teams. Your leaders will face these issues. They are Energy Vampires and the Shining Stars Syndrome.

Energy Vampires

When I speak in front of a group of leaders or conduct strategic workshops for teams to become stronger and more cohesive, it is common for their team to have some type of team member-to-team member interpersonal issue. These types of issues have to be addressed if you want to develop a cohesive team. Oftentimes, this means engaging in the hard work of having the tough conversations and deciding how the team will behave differently in the future. Great teams have those types of conversations. However, at other times, there is significant negativity affecting the team that needs to be addressed directly and simply not allowed any longer.

Jon Gordon, in his book *The Energy Bus*, uses the term "energy vampires" to refer to people who drain your energy as a leader and a team. They are the naysayers, breathing negativity into your teams. Gordon provides the simple prescription for dealing with "energy vampires": don't allow them. After giving them a chance to change, either remove them from the team, or don't include them in anything.

You absolutely must protect the core of the team from "energy vampires." "Energy vampires" are covered in more detail in Part 5: Remove Constraints.

"Shining Stars" Syndrome

We already mentioned the struggle in balancing your star employees with developing teamwork. We love to focus our attention on shining stars. Why not? They get so much done and make us look good!

Josh Bersin, a leading researcher on human resources and performance, says that this is the wrong focus—we get more value from focusing on teams, not just leaders or shining stars.

I call this the "Shining Stars Syndrome."

Remember that everyone today works in a "canoe"—just like my canoe race around the island. In today's workplace, almost no one works as an individual in a vacuum. Therefore, it is just as important to place an emphasis on developing teamwork as it is on developing "shining stars" or individuals.

Please, for the love of all that is good, please stop promoting people with great individual technical skills to leadership positions without additional training.

Look at it another way: "Shining stars" leave when their teams are mediocre. It's just not fun. So, leverage "shining stars" as part of the solution. Get them to help create an environment where performance is much higher, where the bar is raised, where mediocrity is not accepted, where shining stars can shine even brighter. Task them with helping create a team environment.

When they want to do more task work, give them assignments outside the team to stretch and challenge them. That way, the team is still a high priority.

But please, for the love of all that is good, please stop promoting people with great individual technical skills to leadership positions without additional training. Individual contributor vs. team leader roles require completely different skill sets. We get this wrong, and it hurts our organizations.

Don't promote people who are not willing to embrace the team leader role, who don't have this mindset. When you do promote the right people, work with them closely to give them the tools to work collaboratively across functions. You'll do your organization and the people you promote a huge favor.

Remember, except in rare cases, people work in teams. It's teamwork that wins the day.

35

SLOW DOWN TO SPEED UP

THE NORTH SIDE of our house is undeveloped. There is no patio, no nice yard, nothing—just an air conditioning unit, a steep hill that goes down to an occasional creek, and a lot of weeds. Until we develop this side of the house, I need to cut down the weeds every few weeks. It's a long, hot, messy job—but sort of fun—with my gas-powered weed trimmer. The job itself is simple: Turn on the weed trimmer and hack away. In the summer, my primary goal is to get it done quickly because we are in Tennessee and it's hot. I don't want to mess around. I want to get it done.

Occasionally, I get ahead of myself and try to hack into a tall, thick set of weeds that my humble weed trimmer just can't handle. The result is a mess of weeds that are tangled around my trimmer. My trimmer is still somewhat effective but only marginally so. Sometimes I continue to just hack away, even though my performance has literally been cut in half. It is clearly slower, but I just don't want to address the tangled mess. It involves stopping, turning off my trimmer, and cleaning out the tangled mess of weeds. Blah. That's a pain. It takes time. It's easier to just keep hacking away. And so I keep going. I have other things to do, after all.

In reality, it's faster to first slow down and clean up my trimmer.

Most organizations are taking their tangled weed trimmers and just hacking away and telling themselves that they just don't have time to address the tangled mess. There is no time to develop teamwork. They are too busy doing important things. Sometimes, we need to slow down in order to speed up.

During the height of the initial COVID-19 crisis, I was listening to an interview with Michelle Rashid, the Chief Human Resources Officer at Virtuoso, a travel company. If you experienced the lockdowns, you can imagine how a travel company was negatively hit during that crisis. You can imagine the stress on the executive team. You can imagine how important it was to control costs, find sources of revenue, and keep people employed. This is what I was thinking as I listened to her interview. How were they tackling these challenges?

Most organizations are taking their tangled weed trimmers and just hacking away and telling themselves that they just don't have time to address the tangled mess. There is no time to develop teamwork. They are too busy doing important things. Sometimes, we need to slow down in order to speed up.

You can imagine my surprise when Michelle didn't talk about any of them. She talked about what happened when the leadership team recognized that they were not 100 percent aligned, did not have a clear focus, and were not operating as a team. Instead of working harder to find revenue sources and control expenses, they first slowed down. They took time to focus on teamwork and to gain crystal clear alignment around a single goal. That allowed each member of the leadership team to move faster, make decisions more quickly, and adapt more easily to conditions that were changing daily. Perhaps more importantly, it empowered every level below them to do the same.

Michelle described how they slowed down and got messy. Her words were, "When you take the time to slow down and get that clean commitment, you can move a lot faster."

If it's not a pandemic, then there is *no* crisis that is too big to slow down in order to speed up. You'll always be too busy to make sure your teams are right. But it's just an excuse. And that excuse is what separates the best companies from the average ones.

SUMMARY OF KEY POINTS

Individual teams must be highly functional before teams can work with other teams throughout the organization at a high level. It's teamwork that wins the day—not individual skills.

Organizations are shifting to a "network of teams" approach. Success requires a highly functioning *team* of highly functioning *teams.*

The six reasons for mediocre teamwork include:

1. Teamwork is hard, sometimes unrewarding work.
2. We focus on individuals over teams.
3. We leverage contradictory old and new thinking.
4. We misunderstand what it means to be a highly functioning team.
5. We don't have a consistent framework and language to talk about teams and how we work together.
6. The leadership team isn't cohesive.

The four steps to strengthen teams are:

1. Adopt a teamwork framework.
2. Build a cohesive leadership team.
3. Drill teamwork behaviors into every team.
4. Address the common teamwork issues: "energy vampires" and "shining stars syndrome."

It's often critical to slow down in order to speed up.

Visit TheHippoSolution.com/bookresources for assessments, downloads, and additional resources.

IMMEDIATE ACTION STEPS

Take one of these quick action steps to take immediate action:

- <u>Visit the book resource page to assess this variable for your organization.</u>
- <u>Read *The Five Dysfunctions of a Team* by Patrick Lencioni.</u>
- <u>Take a Five Dysfunctions of a Team assessment.</u>
  Visit the book resource page for links and instructions.
- <u>Leverage a team assimilation tool.</u>
  If you are a leader with a new team, leverage a tool to assimilate the team to the new leader faster—and vice versa. Visit the book resource page for recommendations.
- <u>Distribute the three virtues of the ideal team player.</u>
  Give every supervisor, manager, and leader the instructions to conduct The Ideal Team Player exercise by Patrick Lencioni with their team. Visit the book resource page for links and downloads.
- <u>Implement a ten-minute daily check-in with your team.</u>
- <u>Read *The Energy Bus* by Jon Gordon.</u>

Part 4
Eliminate Gaps

"Young hippos can be crushed and killed if they
get caught in the middle of a violent clash
between adult hippos."
—San Diego Zoo

$$\text{The Destination} \times \frac{\text{Individuals} \times \text{Teams} \times \textbf{GAPS}}{\text{Organizational Constraints}}$$

36

THE ACTION IS IN THE GAPS

IT WAS TIME. Looking up from my watch, I forced my weary legs up. It was just past midnight as I began my journey down the hall toward the office where the software developers were working on a last-minute fix. "Hey guys, how's it going?" I asked, feeling apologetic for bugging them for the status yet again. But that was my job as the project manager to coordinate this late-night software release that was strategically important for the company.

"Pretty good."

"Great!" I replied. "When do you think you'll be done?"

"Oh, we finished up about twenty minutes ago. The code is all checked in."

They know that it's past midnight and we all want to go home, right?

"Okay, I'll let the testing folks know."

"Oh, Sonya just popped in here."

"Okay, good."

As I walked back to my office, I knew I should check in with Sonya, just to be sure.

"Hey Sonya. How does it look?"

"How does what look?"

"The updated code."

"What updated code?"

"The updated code the developers checked in twenty minutes ago. They said you just popped in there."

"I did, but they didn't tell me it was ready."

"It's ready."

"Okay, great. Give me fifteen minutes."

Thirteen minutes later, my phone rang.

"Looks great." It was Sonya.

"So, the release folks can run with it?" I asked.

"Yep, good to go," was her reply.

"Okay, thanks."

I went down the hall to the release manager. His job was to place the software release onto the production servers.

"The release is ready."

"Okay, thanks," was his reply, spoken with very little emotion or excitement. I expected a little bit more, like, "Cool, great! I'll get right on it!" or "Finally! It's about time." Instead, "I'll get on it," was his stoic follow-up.

And he did.

Teams can't work well together across the organization unless we eliminate the gaps between them.

The focus of the action is naturally drawn to the tasks that need to be completed and the people completing them. In my example, the developers tended to get the most attention because they were producing the actual product. At the same time, the testers had to ensure that the software was relatively bug-free, and the release managers needed to release it to the world so that customers can use it without interference from pesky issues such as defects, performance problems, or security gaps.

All of that action is important, but equally important is the action in the gaps *between* these different teams and departments. How does information move between these groups? How well do they share information? Are they willing to listen to each other? How do they make decisions together?

Teams can't work well together across the organization unless we eliminate the gaps between them.

37

GAPS ARE EVERYWHERE

DURING A BASKETBALL game, the spectator's focus is on the skill of the players—the ball handlers that cross-over a defender, the deadly three-point shooter, the shot-blocker. Of course, you can't go very far if the individual teammates are not skilled individual players. However, to be a great team, the real action takes place in the gaps between the players. How well do they space the floor, pass the ball, move without the ball, and set their teammates up for a shot?

For a number of years, I sold and implemented software into organizations. The purpose of the software was to get information flowing in the gaps between teams. Of course, software isn't going to make that happen unless the right variables are already in place—it's just a tool—but I certainly understand the motive.

Even as I approached the Air Force base on that Florida morning, there were gaps. If I had been working with the controllers, my mishap would have been prevented—a very simple example of the consequences when there is a gap, a lack of information sharing, between two groups.

It's the same with organizations.

It's in the gaps where the speed, adaptability, resilience, and strength of an organization are determined. It's in the gaps where it's determined how quickly we can "permeate new strategic company objectives" throughout the organization, as PricewaterhouseCoopers articulates it.

This topic right here—teams working together—is the core focus of this book. Not only is it the number one issue that leaders and managers bring up to me, but I saw it in dozens and dozens and dozens of organizations I personally worked with.

While sitting here writing these words, I can look back on just the last two weeks and relay different versions of the same story:

- Different managers and supervisors that have their own methods, practices, and agendas, resulting in their teams unintentionally being pitted against one another
- Different teams that are not willing to help and cross-train with each other
- Teams that resist working together even when a major goal requires collaboration
- Information hitting the wall of a "silo" and simply not passing through that wall

There are many high-profile examples of gaps, such as engineering teams not coordinating together on Boeing's Starliner capsule, resulting in delays and problems. The documentary *Challenger: The Final Flight* documents the sometimes catastrophic results of such gaps. For every high-profile example, there are many, many low-profile yet equally detrimental examples.

Gaps are everywhere.

When I played on our school soccer team in the seventh grade, our coach had a favorite conditioning drill that would pit one player against another. One player would start on one corner of the soccer field. The other player would start on the opposite corner of the same soccer field. When he blew the whistle, we would start running in the same direction. Our goal was to catch the other person while not getting caught ourselves.

You don't have to have played soccer to know that a soccer field is pretty big. I can tell you from personal experience that it's even bigger when you're forced to run around its perimeter.

There were only three possible outcomes from this drill:

1. You caught the other person and could stop running.

2. You were caught by the other person and had to keep running.

3. You threw up.

That's how the people on your teams feel. Even though teams are *technically* "running" in the same direction, they are actually operating alone and positioning themselves against each other so that they look better, never, ever get caught, and, most importantly, don't throw up.

It's like a manager from a large federal agency that spoke up during a leadership meeting I was observing and bravely said, "Why can't we just be one [insert undisclosed agency name]? Why can't we just work together?"

They don't want the organization to be re-structured or the office environment opened up or competition added between teams. They just want to function as a cohesive team.

When I speak to audiences of leaders, this is a fun topic to demonstrate, through interactive activities, both the nature of the problem and how the formula really comes into play. Often, the thinking is solely focused on "breaking down the silos" and getting information flowing. If that is the core focus, it is going to be difficult because it is one-dimensional thinking. You have to think about it multi-dimensionally. For example, if you have established and communicated a distinct destination with a cohesive and aligned leadership team, giving teams a reason to work together, if you have made the lives of your individual people better, if you have strengthened your teams, if you are looking at this multi-dimensionally in the context of the entire formula, this gets much simpler. You've already laid the groundwork.

Even though teams are technically "running" in the same direction, they are actually operating alone and positioning themselves against each other.

Obviously, even when you have laid the groundwork, gaps still don't always close by themselves. It takes intentionality to put in place the right components to eliminate those gaps. When you have laid the groundwork, there are still two components needed to eliminate the gaps between teams.

Before we look at the two components, however, we first need to re-frame the question.

38
REFRAME THE QUESTION

THE QUESTION WE frame is usually around silos—referring to teams that are working in isolation from one another. The question is typically something like, "How do we break down the silos?"

PricewaterhouseCoopers has said that "silos are stubborn obstacles to creating an effective path to growth and profitability." I agree with the substance of this and similar statements; however, I have found that it is helpful to re-frame the question. Here is what I mean. Silos are important. They are good. They provide a home for people—a place where individuals have connections and teammates and comfort. They maximize specializations. They add efficiency. They're healthy. There is a reason you built them in the first place. What we don't want to do is break things apart or reorganize the organization to fix silos and create two to three new problems. Re-organizing may be useful in some cases, but it takes a long time to see benefits. The solution is often much simpler.

The solution is often much simpler. Instead, reframe the question to "How can we eliminate the gaps between the silos?

Instead, re-frame the question to, "How can we eliminate the gaps between the silos?" How can we both maximize the efficiency of each silo while improving the ability of each silo to work *together*? It's like creating a cohesive, fast-moving, quickly adapting "team of silos."

That's our goal.

Now for the two components.

The *Harvard Business Review* reports that there are two problems with teams: They have an us-versus-them mentality, and they have incomplete information. The two components to eliminate the gaps between teams address these two problems. They are:

1. Create authentic relationships between teams.
2. Create collective awareness.

These two components are simple and easy to implement. They focus on changing how people behave, not implementing some fancy cultural initiative or fluffy collaboration language. You can implement these now, today. With intentionality, they will produce results in days so that no one ever thinks or blurts out, "Why can't we just be one [insert your company name]?"

39
COMPONENT #1: CREATE AUTHENTIC RELATIONSHIPS BETWEEN TEAMS

MY VERY FIRST job out of college was as an IT technician and eventually a network administrator for a publishing company. I helped to keep all of the technology running, and I was proud of our team and our work.

One morning, I was called to help a manager who was having a problem with his computer. He was a friendly sort, and as I was working on his computer, we engaged in small talk until he said something that surprised me.

"Hey, did you hear we hired a webmaster?"

My head popped up.

"A webmaster?"

"Yep, he's going to help us move into the digital age."

"Oh?"

This was back at the very beginning of the world wide web when companies were beginning to grapple with if and how this new technology would fit into their businesses. We were no exception. As an IT group, we would occasionally huddle in a conference room to look at this or that website and click around to get ideas for how this technology could work for us. We were taking a lead on it and working to understand it.

We were a centralized IT group supporting three different "companies," one of which now employed the new webmaster.

My first reaction to the news was one of which I am not proud. It wasn't rude or mean so much as it was... protective.

But that's what *our* group does.

You pay *us* to do that.

We're the experts.

That's what *we* are good at.

Won't that make *us* irrelevant?

So you don't like working with *us*?

Why didn't you come talk to *us* first?

A few weeks later, while in some sort of company meeting where new employees were introduced, this gentleman was introduced as "The Webmaster!" A cheer rose up! I felt jealous. Where's the love for all the work *we* do?

At that point in my young career, no one had sat me down and said or intimated that we should control all the technology, that it was our domain, that there were lines in which to stay. Our director certainly wasn't communicating this to us.

The protective reaction just came naturally.

It was a simple, human reaction, an us-versus-them mentality that is all too common.

Whether it is marketing vs. sales, engineering vs. operations, marketing vs. underwriting, IT vs business, or central office vs. the field, we naturally create artificial barriers between ourselves and other teams.

The real problem is that we *artificially* put up barriers between ourselves and other groups, like I did. In a fascinating study by the *South African Journal of Industrial Psychology*, we find that these gaps are artificially created and actually just constructs of our own minds. They are "invisible barriers." We develop our own judgments and perceptions about other people and groups, which affect our behaviors.

Bottom line: Whether it is marketing vs. sales, engineering vs. operations, marketing vs. underwriting, IT vs. business, or central office vs. the field, we naturally create artificial barriers between ourselves and other teams.

Interestingly, we don't put up artificial barriers nearly so much with people on our own teams. We know them, and in many cases—not all—we trust them: They're *our* team. Have you ever watched a football game where the quarterback was hit hard?

His teammates inevitably rise up and protest to the offending player. Why? Because he's on *their* team. He's *their* teammate.

We want the same thing.

To do that, we need to follow human nature and create the same type of relationships.

This is the first component: *Create relationships between teams* (or departments or divisions or silos or whatever distinction you want to insert).

A good, practical goal comes from General Stanley McChrystal in his book *Team of Teams*: for "everyone to know *someone* on every team." What he means is not that everyone knows everyone, but that on each team, there are a number of relationships with members of other teams in the organization. That way, when your team has a need to work with another team or to get information from another team, someone on *your* team already has a relationship with someone on the *other* team.

When there are established relationships, it's harder to develop us-versus-them thinking.

How do we create relationships between different teams? Find a reason for them to do something together.

Ralph Perrey is the Executive Director of the Tennessee Housing Development Agency. His agency does vitally important work to promote the production of affordable housing and preserve and rehabilitate existing housing. Mr. Perrey emphasizes the importance of good leadership practices, such as encouraging candor, making sure everyone understands their role, and catching people doing things well. But he also highlights the importance of frequent, clear communication and deliberate meetings to develop "smoother working relationships" between business units. This has become especially important for his agency because it is launching more and more initiatives that require multiple business units to work together in order for those initiatives to be successful. I suspect your organization is experiencing something similar.

40
METHODS OF CREATING AUTHENTIC RELATIONSHIPS

HERE ARE SOME examples for how to practically develop those relationships.

Forums

Plan regular forums for people from multiple teams to get together and talk about something meaningful. For example, the British Society for Immunology held a forum with representatives from multiple departments to share views on inflammation. You could plan a forum to talk about how to improve your engineering process or how to improve customer service or how to get everyone involved in marketing. Better yet, empower them to make decisions or craft recommendations.

Cross-Integrated Groups

In a situation where certain teams must work together, create a group of individuals from each of the individual teams that meets regularly. The goal of the integrated team could be to solve problems for members of each of the individual teams, coordinate efforts, and share information.

Heather Gahir, Ph.D., is the Vice President of Talent Strategy and Organizational Development for Jackson National Life Insurance Company. According to Gahir, "It's especially difficult for teams to work together when they have common responsibilities. When their scope is clearly different, it's easier." In this type of situation, she recommends creating a group of individuals from the teams that need to work together. The purpose of this group is to solve problems for the two teams. For example, if a member of one team needs access to a resource and can't get it, they can put it in the queue for this cross-integrated group to solve. If the group cannot solve the issue, they can bump it up to a higher power or to the teams themselves. "In my experience, this works best and is faster than waiting for the results of a restructuring."

Integrated Group Lunches

Integrated group lunches are as simple as what a hospital I worked with does: Their leaders are broken up into smaller groups and placed with others they may not work with on a regular basis. They meet together, many times just for lunch. The goal is to get to know other leaders.

Leader Lunches

Leader lunches create relationships and close the gaps between two leaders by getting them to spend more time together. A leader lunch is simply spending regular time with another leader from another team or department to talk through your perspectives and differences. It's a valuable leadership rhythm that has been leveraged by many leaders to create relationships between not just the leaders but the departments they represent. Model it yourself and encourage your direct reports to do the same.

Intentionally invite leaders with whom you do not see eye to eye as well as leaders you wouldn't think about asking to lunch. Perhaps they have a different background or style or personality. Look for leaders that, for whatever reason, you may not initially think to invite.

Work-Outs

Jack Welch championed the Work-Out approach at GE almost 30 years ago. When there was an issue that needed to be resolved or a solution found, a "Work-Out" session would physically bring together key people from various functions with a neutral facilitator. Today, of course, while in-person is best, you could do it virtually. They would form a small group to explore various alternative options and come up with a solution. This was just part of their culture. You can use a similar approach to get people working and creating solutions *together*. Google "Jack Welch" and "Work-Out," and you'll find a wealth of information to get you started.

If you leverage this type of approach and there are some politics at play, you may also benefit from advice by PricewaterhouseCoopers: Have a neutral facilitator or consider employing co-leaders (otherwise, the group may be misunderstood and not trusted). And pay attention to the group size—too large of a group dilutes decision-making.

Rotating Jobs

Disney is an example of an organization where people rotate jobs—in their case, every two years. There are multiple benefits: There are always people you know or worked with on other teams, it breaks down the us-versus-them mentalities, and you don't get too comfortable and narrowly focused staying at the same place.

Many other organizations employ a similar tactic. Various agencies in the United States Federal Government rotate leadership posts regularly. Nissan North America has a program in which rising managers rotate job assignments between different departments and organizations. Managers then become leaders who already have relationships and experience in multiple departments and organizations.

Required Training

Many organizations have training requirements, whether they involve compliance, safety, ethics, regulatory, or whatever. Never just look at this as simply training. This is a prime opportunity for relationship-building. If every participant has not connected with other participants from other teams in the "class" and walked away with some new relationships, you've lost a golden opportunity. Build in time for intentional networking and working together on training exercises in order to build relationships. This one is easy because you have to do it anyway. All it takes is just a little more intentionality. I know that many of these types of trainings are online or in an eLearning format. Even then, simply insert an assignment to work with someone else to come up with an answer to a problem, or interview someone to see how this applies to their department—anything!

Visit Other Departments

Schedule some time for representatives of teams to regularly visit other teams and departments to learn what they do and vice versa. HCA Healthcare does this. They periodically take members of their IT team to visit clinical settings so they learn how people are using their technology tools. At the same time, they are developing relationships with people in those clinical departments.

Briefs and Debriefs

In his book *Fearless Success*, John Foley, a former Blue Angels pilot, emphasizes how important briefs and debriefs are to a team's success. With the right parameters, they can be valuable tools to bring different teams together to work on getting better. Leverage these for projects, milestones, deliverables, events, and launches on which multiple teams are working. Read Foley's book to learn how the Blue Angels conduct their briefs and debriefs.

Joint Training

Some organizations conduct joint training exercises. The military comes to mind. They train jointly with other services, other groups, sometimes even other countries. In addition to benefiting from the training itself, it builds relationships that are key for people to break down those artificial barriers and create a desire to work with one another. It builds camaraderie as well as sharpens skills.

Don't forget to include briefs and debriefs—that's where you'll find much of the magic happening.

Cross-Utilization Assignments

Place people in temporary assignments in other teams and departments. Have them work embedded for two weeks/two months/six months. This is real work, not just observational. Doing someone else's job changes your perspective. Disney is an example of a company that implements this model.

Your original reaction might be "no way we're doing that," maybe because you believe that "we can't lose this person" or "that would disrupt everything." Rethink it. This is a powerful tool. Not only will your team members have a much clearer understanding of what is done and how, but they will have established deeper relationships with that other team. The other team will benefit from the thinking brought in by the newly embedded team member and vice versa. It's powerful. Don't send your weakest employee. Send your strongest.

These examples should spark your thinking. The question now is: What could you do to build relationships between teams? It doesn't have to be complicated or time-consuming. It just takes intentionality.

41

COMPONENT #2:
CREATE COLLECTIVE AWARENESS

"CESSNA 180 PAPA Alpha, traffic is at 4:00, a Boeing 737 on a four mile final to runway 01."

My instructor and I whipped our heads to the right and there they were: the landing lights of a Boeing 737 airliner that looked awfully bright and awfully *close*. I'm sure the pilots of that 737 were more than a little concerned that they were flying anywhere in the vicinity of our little four-seat Cessna 172.

"Cessna 180 Papa Alpha, this isn't going to work. Make a left 360-degree turn."

My instructor in the right seat turned the yoke to the left and quickly started a full 360-degree turn to allow for spacing between ourselves and the 737 jet, which was landing on an intersecting runway. My instructor was "driving" because I was not experienced enough for this level of intensity.

"Nice job, Cessna 180 Papa Alpha!" the controller exclaimed after my instructor had almost finished his turn. "Cleared to land runway 04."

And so he did.

We landed at Reagan National Airport in Washington and headed to the general aviation terminal to pick up my instructor's mom who had just flown in to visit.

It was a fun, intense experience that I will never forget because it gave me a real appreciation for the communication and the level of situational awareness that are necessary to fly safely and capably.

Communicating and situational awareness are two skills that are just as important as flying the actual airplane. In fact, you cannot earn a pilot's license without them.

You have to effectively communicate with air traffic control (ATC) to inform them exactly where you are and where you are going. You have to interpret their instructions and follow them. You have to talk to other airplanes, especially when you are flying into or out of an airport that does not have a control tower.

You have to take that information and constantly create a mental picture of your location, the location of every other plane, and where everyone will be in the near future. All of this is to create a collective awareness so that everyone can properly and safely complete their flight. Your teams need the same level of situational awareness, which brings us to the second component to eliminate gaps between teams: create collective awareness.

The Problem

Teams don't work well together if they don't know what other teams are doing. I didn't need to know all of the details of what other pilots were doing in their own cockpits, but I did need to have a good general picture of where they were and where they were going. Same for teams. I don't need to know everything that every other team is doing. I do need to have a good general picture of what every other team is doing. Otherwise, teams tend to focus on their own agendas, their own goals, and their own initiatives, which is like flying without communicating.

Focusing on your own agenda may work fine for individual team projects. However, when the activity and intensity increases, when initiatives require coordination, when conditions are changing quickly, when you need to think bigger, when decisions need to be made now, when change needs to be coordinated, if everyone does not have that collective awareness, you are inevitably going to run into the other "planes." As one person put it in a recent session of mine, "You're going to have a lot of sheet metal strewn around the ground."

We've all experienced the lack of collective awareness. Even my nephew, only a few years into his career, has experienced it. When I explained to him the premise for this book, his response was, "Oh yeah, we need better teamwork. We have no idea what other teams are doing." Indeed.

The Solution

"There's another one," I remarked after hearing the radio call. I strained my neck looking through the windshield, trying to locate the airplane that may be intersecting our flight path. Accidentally flying into another airplane was not on my list of things to do this Saturday.

"There he is," I said. "He won't be a factor." We continued on.

The radio chatter was consistent as we flew across middle Tennessee, heading back home. It required vigilance to make sure that we did not intersect another airplane's flight path.

This time, it wasn't me sitting in the pilot's seat. It was my son, who had recently earned *his* pilot's license. I was just along for the ride. Unlike my trip to Washington Reagan Airport years ago, this radio chatter was because we were flying past several uncontrolled airports and airspace in this part of the state. There are no air traffic controllers to guide us here.

However, there is a handy tool that makes it a lot easier: the common traffic advisory frequency. It is a single radio frequency that every airplane uses in uncontrolled airspace to call out where they are, at which altitude they are flying, and where they are going. It provides every other airplane in the area awareness and a mental picture of what's going on around them. Multiple airports use it. Every airplane in the vicinity uses it. As my son and I flew across middle Tennessee, all we had to do was listen to that frequency to maintain awareness.

Your teams need a "common traffic advisory frequency." The goal is not for every team to know every detail of what every other team is doing. The goal is to give every team a mental picture of what's happening across the organization.

General McChrystal calls this "shared consciousness." *Harvard Business Review* dubbed this a "shared mindset." I call it "collective awareness."

A word of caution: For whatever reason, we all develop a tendency to withhold information. It makes me think of Emily Dickinson's poem "Tell all the Truth but tell it slant." So remember Bethune's law of communication: Unless it's dangerous or illegal to share, we share it. Otherwise, teams will inevitably run into each other, or worse, expend needless energy doing needless activities. The benefits of sharing far, far outweigh the risks.

The goal is not for every team to know every detail of what every other team is doing. The goal is to give every team a mental picture of what's happening across the organization.

How do we create this collective awareness?

Simple. Put in place a rhythm to share information: a regular, constant source of information in which everyone participates to both share and receive information.

42
METHODS OF CREATING COLLECTIVE AWARENESS

YOU WILL HAVE to create your own rhythm that makes sense for your business and culture. Naturally, I cannot tell you exactly what that rhythm should be. What I can do is provide several examples to spark your thinking. Adopt one of these examples or use them as a spark to create your own.

Alan Mulally's Business Process Review

Every Thursday for two hours, Alan's management team would meet to review the business. By "management team," don't think just a handful of people. There were a lot of people in this meeting to be sure that every team knew what was going on.

They would start with a review of the overall plan. Every person knew the plan. It wasn't complicated. In fact, the plan fit on a business card-size piece of paper. During the Thursday meeting, each leader would report on their part of the plan, including a color coding to designate their current status.

When he started this rhythm, it took a while before leaders had the confidence to be vulnerable and share what was really going on. Mulally has told the story of how he clapped when the first red status finally appeared. Mulally says that, "If it's not a shared environment, people are not going to have the confidence to share how it's really going. Then you're just managing a secret—you don't know what's going on."

This level of awareness and information-sharing turned Mulally's organization into a cohesive network of teams that was working toward a common goal: the survival and turnaround of Ford Motor Company, in this case. Teams could see what other teams were doing. Teams would start to offer help to other teams that needed it. It became a true "team of teams."

And it worked. Ford Motor Company turned around.

The War Room

David Fox has been an executive focused on customer-focused cultures for over twenty years. One day, as he was driving to the office, he received a phone call from a colleague telling him about a system issue. As soon as he arrived, David sprinted into the building, bypassed his office without checking email, grabbing coffee, or chatting with co-workers, and ran up two flights of stairs into the company's war room. Thankfully, he arrived just before the CEO, who looked at David and said, "Where is everybody else?"

You see, when there was an issue, every executive was expected to be in the war room, focused on the issue until it was resolved. The war room was a physical room lined with computers and monitors so that every executive and manager had all of the information necessary to solve the problem quickly. The war room was not just active during an issue—it was active 24/7. The war room constantly provided the information needed for everyone to create a great customer experience. The war room provided collective awareness.

You could employ a similar approach.

By the way, don't miss a key insight from his story.

You see, David's story not only illustrates the use of a war room but reveals an important truth for what actually made the war room effective: the CEO's hyper-focus on a great customer experience. Sure, the war room was a method to achieve the goal but would not have been effective without the clear focus on what was more important than anything else: providing a great customer experience. It was a clear reference point, a distinct destination and articulation about what was ultimately most important for the organization.

If you put two variables of the formula together—a clear reference point and a method of providing collective awareness to achieve it—like David's CEO did, you start to unlock the power of the formula.

Intentional Leadership Rhythms

An executive with a nationally recognized insurance company relayed to me how they conduct weekly CEO meetings with senior leadership, bi-weekly meetings with mid-level leadership, and monthly meetings with everyone. It's a good example of an intentional leadership rhythm to create collective awareness.

1x1 Meetings

Don't forget the power of your 1x1 meetings with direct reports. Leverage them to drill into their heads the need to share information proactively.

Rebecca Hunter, former Chief Human Resources Officer for 40,000+ employees in the State of Tennessee government, says that the reason why people don't share information and work together across teams is usually *not* because people flat-out refuse to share information. While that certainly occurs, more often than not, people don't share information and work together because they just don't think about it.

Hunter emphasizes the importance of one-on-one meetings with her immediate team. During these meetings, she routinely asks the question: "Who else needs to know what you know?" She does this because she's found that people just didn't think about sharing information. They weren't against sharing it, they were just busy and focused on their own work, which is why she continuously ingrained the concept of sharing information and collaborating with other people—inside and outside their team boundary—who "need to know."

NASA's Teleservices Network

Everyone knows about the tremendous success of the Apollo project back in the 1960s and 1970s. What you may not know is how collective awareness played a significant role in its success. As described in his book *Team of Teams*, General McChrystal explains how NASA brought in George Mueller to connect their teams. He built a "teleservices network" to connect engineers and managers from NASA and different contractor organizations. They would simply tune in to the real-time feed.

How can you create a continuous cross-feed across your teams that need to work together? I don't mean just passing information—I mean data plus real human-to-human interaction. Of course, we have tremendous technology platforms to aid in this today, such as Slack, Microsoft Teams, and a myriad of other tools. You could set up a regular Zoom meeting that runs every day at a specified time, perhaps even continuously, depending on your project and domain. Just remember, it's not just data—the key is to facilitate real human-to-human interaction.

Daily Check-In/Check-Out

Software development teams often employ a habit of conducting a daily ten-minute standing meeting. Usually, these are in the mornings so that everyone knows what everyone is doing, what the issues are, and what the plan for the day is.

Daily check-outs at the end of the day can also be helpful, especially if many are working remotely: what happened, what was done, what remains, what is the plan for tomorrow, what's most important? Consider implementing your own daily check-in/check-out, perhaps even with a broader audience.

This type of constant communication is important, even if you don't think you need it.

Heather Gahir, Ph.D., Vice President of Talent Strategy and Organizational Development for Jackson National Life Insurance Company, emphasizes this when she says that "It is important to have intense communication while you are figuring out how to get teams to work together. You have to keep people in communication with each other. That's where collaboration breaks down: because they don't communicate with each other often enough."

The Scoreboard

Sometimes, collective awareness can be physical in nature. A couple of years ago, I visited a Lifeway Christian Resources distribution center. I remember the big electronic scoreboard on the wall that told every single person in the building what was going on, what the goals were, how much had been accomplished, and what was left to be done. All they had to do was look up. It's not unlike my basketball teams—we could always look up on the wall and know *exactly* where we stood. How could you implement a similar resource, such as a balanced scorecard?

Time Outs

If you are going 100 percent and never have a "time out," you will not reach your destination, at least not without completely wearing yourself out.

When I coach basketball, we could have the best plan, but the other team doesn't always do their part and let us execute the plan. We get out of our rhythm, get flustered, or lose our focus. That's where time outs come in. It's an opportunity to reset. Sometimes, we just needed to get back to the plan. Sometimes, we needed to adapt the plan. But we often needed to step back and reset.

If you are going 100 percent and never have a "time out," you will not reach your destination, at least not without completely wearing yourself out. Implement "time outs."

These time outs could be retreats, leadership meetings, offsites, weekly debriefs. These are not team-building activities. You may employ some team-building during your "time out," but it's important to re-establish collective awareness: What is our plan, what is most important, what are the current realities and issues, what do we need to change, and how do we move forward?

Software Productivity Tools

Software productivity tools are not effective.

Gulp.

I personally developed project management/productivity tools for teams, and I believe in them, so hear me out.

If you want people to work together, you have to insist that they work together.

For our purposes here, we need collective awareness— what everyone else is doing, how that fits into the vision, what the issues are. That is best done live, person to person, with real human interaction. Not necessarily in-person—virtual can work—but live.

There is absolutely no substitute: If you want people to work together, you have to insist that they work together. Not typing words into a software system. They need to hear each other, ask questions, even challenge each other.

There is no substitute for people actually working together.

Having said that, software productivity tools have their place. They are great at managing the actual detail and execution of what was decided. Use them for managing tasks that have to be done that day, notifying people when tasks are done and their tasks can begin, tracking issues in a central location so they don't get lost, recognizing how much work everyone has, interacting with questions on how to complete a task, etc. These are related to execution *after* teams have higher-level clarity and awareness. Software productivity tools should be used to track and document the teamwork, not build it.

Let me give you an example. Army tanks have sophisticated technology systems that link tanks together, meaning every tank commander knows exactly where their fellow tanks are on the battlefield. It's a technology tool that gives them a clear picture and advantage as they are executing the battle plan. But that is not a substitute for the discussion that takes place to create the battle plan, to provide updates as to each tank and commander's intentions, and to make decisions and adapt as the battle unfolds. In other words, the tool greatly helps the execution—it's not a substitute for the conversation.

I cannot stress enough that working together is a multi-dimensional issue. You have to consider all of the vari-

> *Software productivity tools should be used to track and document the teamwork, not build it.*

ables of the formula. If you just start throwing people in a room and expect them to use one of these formats to start working together, good luck. If your people do not understand that debate around ideas is critical as one of the key behaviors of a high-functioning team, this is going to be difficult. If they do not have clarity on what is most important, this isn't going to work, because everyone is looking through a different lens. When you consider the entire formula and work on the other elements, this becomes much, much easier.

SUMMARY OF KEY POINTS

The real action that dictates an organization's health, speed, and ability to adapt is in the gaps between teams. Teams can't work well together unless we eliminate the gaps between teams and departments.

Reframe the question from "How do we break down silos?" to "How do we eliminate the gaps between silos?" When the rest of the formula is put in place, there are two components needed to eliminate the gaps between teams:

- Creating real relationships between teams
- Creating collective awareness across the organization

Visit TheHippoSolution.com/bookresources for assessments, downloads, and additional resources.

IMMEDIATE ACTION STEPS

Take one of these quick action steps to take immediate action:

- Visit the book resource page to assess this variable for your organization.
- Read *Silos, Politics, and Turf Wars* by Patrick Lencioni with your leadership team.
- Ask another leader, with whom you don't agree, to lunch once a week for the next month.
- Schedule a forum around a specific topic important to multiple teams.
- Schedule a Work-Out session with representatives from multiple groups to solve a particular problem.
- Start your own Business Process Review.

  Leverage Alan Mulally's model and invite more leaders and managers to join a weekly review meeting. Encourage vulnerability, information sharing, and helping each other.

Part 5
Remove Constraints

"Hippos defecate so much that sometimes
all of the fish in the river die."
—The Atlantic

$$\text{The Destination} \times \frac{\text{Individuals} \times \text{Teams} \times \text{Gaps}}{\textbf{ORGANIZATIONAL CONSTRAINTS}}$$

43
OVER THE TREES

I COULD FEEL the rumble as my son held the brakes and revved up the engine before we took off from Sewanee, Tennessee. That's a normal practice for gas-powered airplane engines—rev them up temporarily to make sure that the engine is working properly before you take off. There's only one engine, after all, and in this case, we really needed it to work because there was a forest of tall trees a mere 2,524 feet past the end of the runway.

My hands became just a little bit sweaty. Telling my son, who was flying the plane, that I trusted in his piloting skills became... a little more real.

We had flown into this airport at the top of the Cumberland Plateau two hours prior. It had been an enjoyable, sunny, early morning flight. Sewanee is a fun little airport with forest on all four sides. It's beautiful.

After you land, however, the view looks a little different, a little more foreboding staring at those trees from ground level. The runway doesn't look quite as spacious as it did from the air.

After we landed, we had walked about a mile into town on a forest-covered trail for some breakfast and coffee. It was delightful. I even picked up some fresh corn on the cob at a farmer's market on the walk back to the airport.

But now, we had to take off and head back home. My son advanced the throttle, and the engine roared to life again. This time, he let the brakes go, and we started down the runway. Before I knew it, my son pulled the stick back, raising the nose of the plane, and up we went.

My son's eyes darted between the nose of the plane and the instruments. My eyes were glued to the trees. I knew we would make it—we had enough space for the airplane to do its thing. At least... yeah, yeah, we would make it.

Right after we lifted off the ground, my son did something expected but disconcerting. He lowered the nose. I gulped, even though I knew it was coming. There was a reason he did this. The tendency is to pull back on the stick just a little too much, approach the trees just a little too slow, and leave yourself with very little margin, or worse—you stall and crash because you were so focused on clearing the trees. Neither one of us wanted that. The idea is to lower the nose a bit to gain speed, then pull back to climb. That way, you both climb more quickly and you have enough speed to handle any unexpected wind or downdrafts so that you don't get into a dangerously slow situation.

Sure enough, after a few long seconds, our speed increased, and he pulled back more on the stick. Up we went.

My eyes were still glued to the trees as we reached the edge of the forest with plenty of room to spare. Just like he planned it. I knew all along we'd make it, of course.

Here's the truth of the matter: If we took off from that airport one hundred times, we should safely clear the trees every single time. There is no reason there should ever be any doubt. The reason is that there are specific performance charts, formulas, and calculations you run so that you know how the plane will perform based on variables such as weight, runway length, wind, altitude, and temperature.

That statement, however, assumes that all of your systems are functioning properly. If any of those systems were not operating at peak performance, we would have been in trouble.

If the engine wasn't producing the power it was rated to produce, we wouldn't have had enough speed or performance to clear the trees.

If the airspeed indicator wasn't working correctly, we would not have known our true airspeed, which would have created a dangerous situation.

Most importantly of all, if the pilot was fatigued, too inexperienced, didn't know the correct procedures, didn't properly evaluate the impact of wind and weather, didn't properly estimate the performance ahead of time, or didn't adequately assess the risk, we would be in trouble.

If the organizational systems around teams are not operating properly, your teams won't work together.

It's the same thing with teams working together in organizations. We have this wonderful formula to get teams working together. Of course, it's not that easy, is it? Organizations are filled with people, each with passions and emotions and behaviors. Organizations are filled with systems and processes—some of which have been around for a long time. There are naturally going to be problems—both interpersonal and organizational.

If the airplane systems were not working properly, we wouldn't have made it over the trees. If the organizational systems around teams are not operating properly around them, your teams won't work together. They won't make it "over the trees." They won't be productive and execute at a high level.

44

THE FIVE CONSTRAINTS

WHEN I WORK with senior leadership teams, sometimes the issue lies here: The leadership team has done the right things to foster organizational teamwork, but there are organizational constraints tugging the other way. Because of these constraints, the leadership team just can't seem to make steady progress.

Harvard Business Review calls this having a supportive context. How does the organization support teams working together?

I call it organizational constraint: How are the natural workings of the organization constraining teams from working together?

Why is this so important? Because teams can't be productive with these constraints pulling on them. It's no fun. It sucks the joy out of the experience. Constraints cause an enormous expenditure of time and energy. We become entangled in the constraints instead of being productive and executing together at a high level.

Each variable of the formula so far has been a multiplier, meaning that when you focus on and improve a variable, they have a multiplier effect throughout the organization. But this variable is a divisor, it negates the power of the other variables. It's like gravity to flight or ice cream to weight loss.

We must remove these constraints.

There are five common organizational constraints that have a negative effect on teams working together:

1. Energy vampires
2. Incongruent rewards
3. Poor treatment of others
4. Bloated decision-making
5. Unequipped leaders

We'll look at them one at a time. The goal is not to transform every constraint. The goal is to find the one or two constraints that are having a major impact right now on how your teams are or are not working together.

By applying energy toward fixing that constraint, it unleashes the multiplying power of the rest of the formula.

45
CONSTRAINT #1: ENERGY VAMPIRES

JON GORDON USES the term "energy vampires" in his book *The Energy Bus* to refer to people who drain your energy. They are the naysayers, breathing negativity into your teams. They could be the people who simply will not collaborate or are resistant to change.

You know who these people are. You don't enjoy being around them. You and your team members feel drained of energy after you are around them. You'd rather avoid them. You may even wish they weren't there.

John Maxwell, in his book *The 17 Indisputable Laws of Teamwork*, talks about how your team's strength is impacted by its weakest link and how the team is not for everyone.

Gordon provides the prescription for dealing with "energy vampires": Don't allow them. After giving them a legitimate chance to change, either remove them from the team, or don't include them in the team's initiatives. Don't let them drain the energy from the rest of the team. You have to protect the core of the team.

There are two reasons that "energy vampires" flourish.

First, we don't want to have the difficult conversation. Michael Brody-Waite, in his book *Great Leaders Live Like Drug Addicts*, says that most leaders are sitting on a difficult conversation. We don't want to have the conversation, so we let the behavior flourish to the detriment of both individual teams and the "team of teams."

When I speak, sometimes I will leverage a case study technique using audience members to demonstrate the idea of "energy vampires." It's fun because most everyone can relate to both the issue of "energy vampires" as well as our reluctance to have the difficult conversation. We have to be able to have the difficult conversation with those whose negativity is affecting teams. We have to directly say that negative behavior and energy is not allowed. While there are many models and tools for having difficult conversations, such as the Center for Creative Leadership's Situation-Behavior-Impact model, the best piece of advice I have received is simple: Don't hesitate, and start the conversation off with a firm statement on what needs to change. Just get to it.

Second, we spend too much energy and time giving "energy vampires" attention. The Law of Thirds helps with this. I learned this model from Patrick Lencioni, though he is not its creator. You have three groups of people in your organization: supporters, naysayers, and undecideds. We tend to give more energy and time to the naysayers because they tend to be more vocal and demanding. Instead, focus your energy and time on supporters, not on the naysayers. That will encourage the supporters, causing them to stay engaged and not leave, while causing the undecideds to become supporters because they see that's how to get attention. Focusing on supporters will also cause naysayers to change their behavior or leave.

The big takeaway is that you can't allow "energy vampires." You must have the tough conversation. Otherwise, it will destroy your ability to develop cohesive, productive teams that work together at a high level.

46
CONSTRAINT #2: INCONGRUENT REWARDS

WHEN I WAS a kid, one summer I attended what was commonly called a Vacation Bible School. During that week, there was a competition to see who could memorize the largest number of Bible verses. I have always loved a good competition, so when we received a sheet of paper with several dozen verses to memorize, I started to memorize. I don't remember how many I learned. I know I learned more verses than anyone else.

On the final evening, there was an awards ceremony. I was standing on the stage with many of the other kids as different award winners were announced. I waited with anticipation.

Finally, after waiting for what seemed like an eternity, it was time for my award: most memorized verses. I got ready to walk forward.

I listened as a description of the award was given. "And now, the person who memorized the most verses this week was..." My foot moved forward half a step before I realized that it was not my name that was called. I was dumbfounded. The girl who was named only memorized about half the number of verses that I did. I know because she told me. I was perplexed. While I am usually very reserved, I remember that my eyes began to water. I couldn't understand it. I was upset. I did what was asked. What happened?

Heidi Gardner with *Harvard Business Review* tells a similar story of a business leader who adopted the mantra of his CEO for people and teams to collaborate with each other. And so the leader did what I would have done, exactly what the CEO requested: He collaborated with others.

At the end of the year, the business leader was at his awards ceremony, not unlike when I was in grade school. He did not receive a single award, while he watched person after person being rewarded and recognized for achieving individual goals and accomplishments. Nothing about collaborating.

I do not know what the leader felt in that moment, but I suspect it was similar to what I felt standing on that stage in grade school. And I'll bet he resolved, like I did, to never get suckered again.

Reward systems are typically individual- and department-oriented. Each individual's compensation is tied to their individual performance. They may have SMART (specific, measurable, achievable, realistic, timely) goals that they need to meet or certain performance metrics, such as a sales person who has to meet a certain sales quota or a customer service representative who has to meet certain call quotas. Your SMART goals may even have team, division, or department components.

You can create the best mantras, the best plan, the best vision for the future, perhaps even a contest or a pretty banner hung in the lunchroom. You could go all-in communicating how people need to work together and focus on a particular change. But if a salesperson is compensated by meeting their quota, then meeting their quota will be their priority, regardless of your pretty little change. If a team member has a SMART goal of partnering with a sister agency but their compensation or bonus or recognition is tied to their productivity within the department, then guess what's going to happen?

Sales departments are typically rewarded by the sales they produce. Engineering departments are rewarded by their productivity or quality. Marketing departments are typically rewarded by the success of their marketing campaigns, and so on. Each department has their own individual measurements. No manager within a department will prioritize working together with teams in other departments if they are being measured and compensated mostly by what they produce for their own department.

So what do we need to do?

Implement collective rewards that reward everyone for working together.

If something is rewarded, you get more of it.

There are a myriad of ideas for collective rewards from which to choose, many of which are contextual to your business and the direction you are attempting to implement.

For example, when I worked for a manufacturing company, we were rewarded with prizes, praise, and bonuses for collectively achieving ISO certification. It demanded that we all worked together to establish proper quality systems. It worked.

If something is rewarded, you get more of it.

Rewards do not need to be just monetary, nor should they be. You can reward people with team or group recognition, more responsibility, and any number of creative alternatives. Thinking creatively is usually required at first because changing compensation strategy usually takes a lot of time. While monetary rewards should be considered, they may not always even be the best course of action.

Forbes provides several examples in the areas of financial, experiential, and public recognition rewards such as tablets, gadgets, bonuses based on helping other employees improve their careers, and team dinners with top executives.

Make it easy for people to do the right thing.

Don't overthink it. Put yourself in the role of leaders and managers. How will they feel at the year-end award ceremony? Even better, ask them. Learn what would motivate them. Make it easy for people to do the right thing.

Oh, are you wondering why I lost the verse competition? So was I. It turns out there was a rule that I never heard about and that wasn't on the paper I received. It was a "hidden" rule. We were supposed to memorize verses *in order.* On a purely personal note: Please don't have silly, unwritten rules that accompany your rewards.

47
CONSTRAINT #3:
POOR TREATMENT OF OTHERS

WHILE I WAS in college, I took a temporary job with Manpower, a temporary employment agency. One of my first assignments was in an engineering office. I do not remember the name of the company. I do not remember what the company produced. I do not remember the products that this particular group was engineering. I do remember how two different managers treated me.

The first individual asked me to copy and distribute some reports. After placing a rubber

I remember how I was treated more than 30 years later.

band around the reports, as directed, I remember this individual yelling at me because the rubber band caused the papers to bend.

The second individual also gave me assignments but was kind and even called me into his office to apologize for the behavior of the first individual.

I remember how I was treated more than 30 years later.

There are two manifestations of how we treat each other that affects how teams work together:

1. Treating people with unkindness and disrespect
2. Stifling interactions

Both of them constrain teams from being cohesive and constrain teams from working together with other teams in the organization.

Manifestation #1: Treating people with unkindness and disrespect

My story about the two managers is an example of treating people with unkindness and disrespect. If my experience was the exception, there would be no reason to write about it. But it's not.

There is never a reason not to treat people with kindness and respect.

Michael Abrashoff, in his book *It's Your Ship*, wrote how he realized that people had been leaving the Navy—and his ship in particular—because they were not being treated with dignity and respect and because they were being prevented from making an impact on the organization.

In my career, I have physically been in the offices and meetings of dozens and dozens and dozens of companies, and that doesn't count the many more that I have interacted with virtually or over the phone. While there are many kind and respectful managers and leaders, there are many instances where unkindness and disrespect is tolerated. Sometimes it is overt. Many times it is subtle.

Being kind and respectful does not mean you cannot be direct and have passionate debate. You can be direct while being calm, kind, and respectful.

There is never a reason not to treat people with kindness and respect.

I have made two related observations over the years.

The first observation is that being kind and respectful does not mean you cannot be direct and have passionate debate. You can be direct while being calm, kind, and respectful. A leader must at times be direct; otherwise, poor performance and behavior are allowed to continue. It is necessary to say "that's not good enough" or "you cannot behave that way." But it should always be done in a kind, respectful, professional way.

It is also important for team members to conduct passionate debate with each other around ideas, but that can all be done with professionalism, kindness, and respect.

Dr. Paul Sternberg, Chief Medical Officer for Vanderbilt University Medical Center, emphasizes the importance of self-awareness. "You can only evolve if you are aware of what you are trying to do," he says. There was a time earlier in his career when he was recruited for various leadership positions. While he was enamored, he turned them down until he felt that he was a little more mature.

When he finally moved into senior leadership, he articulates how he knew that he couldn't behave in the same way. He couldn't have a short fuse but needed to be the calmest person in the world.

It's an excellent example of how the leader sets the tone.

The second observation is that it isn't so much that leaders don't recognize that there is poor behavior so much as they don't want to have the difficult conversation. Not only are difficult conversations needed for "energy vampires," they are also needed for unprofessional, disrespectful, unkind behavior.

> *"Words spoken by kind people have the ability to endure in our lives." —Bob Goff*

Unkind and disrespectful behavior cannot be tolerated. It's a deal-breaker. It zaps people's energy, causes them to pull back, and reduces morale.

Alan Mulally, the former CEO of Ford and Boeing Commercial Airplanes, whose principles we have referenced before, is very clear on this point. People must treat each other with respect. It's non-negotiable. No one gets to violate that rule. It's the right thing to do.

As Bob Goff wrote in his book *Love Does,* "Words spoken by kind people have the ability to endure in our lives."

Manifestation #2: Stifling interactions

Earlier in my career, when my immediate manager was moved to another client, I was suddenly thrust into the role of managing the year 2000 testing project for a hospital in the Northwest. The goal of these projects was to ensure that critical computer systems continued to operate normally after January 1, 2000. I was technically a consultant with the local office of a consulting company, hired by the hospital to handle their year 2000 testing.

After being placed in my new role, not only did I need to think about my testing team, but I had to become aware of a much wider operation. You see, this hospital was part of a system of hospitals, each of which had a team of consultants conducting year 2000 testing for their particular hospital.

Each of these efforts was ultimately overseen by the regional CIO for the hospital system.

One day, I emailed the regional CIO with some insights that I thought needed to be considered. I do not remember the details of the email, except that they were not exceptional. They were simple, straightforward considerations.

I got reprimanded. Not by the CIO but by my boss, who indicated that she was going to have to contact the regional CIO and "fix this."

Interestingly, I found out later that the regional CIO appreciated my contributions. I understand what my boss was doing—she was responsible for managing this important client relationship, and technically, there was a chain of command. She had other nuances to consider of which I was probably not aware. She had a much broader picture. I get it—she was doing her job, and she was a great boss for which to work.

The point is that while the reprimand was minor in reality, it had an immediate impact. I became reticent to communicate to anyone outside of my immediate team and boss. I became reticent to express new ideas and observations that didn't fit with the standard narrative. I still remember it. That's just human nature.

Even if the reprimand was necessary, be careful about the result on future interactions. Be clear about how the flow of information and communication should work.

This is an example of how we interact with each other. If people have unwritten rules to follow, however well-intentioned and perhaps even necessary, the free flow of information and collaboration between individuals on different teams will slow down and eventually stop.

Obviously, this point varies by your domain. Some domains have security, regulatory, or other considerations, but for most domains, understand that stifling interactions constrain teams from working together across the organization.

What can you do if you are inheriting an organization that has not treated people well or you are now realizing that there are subtle ways in which people are not treating each other as they should? Here are three very simple ideas that you can implement today.

Write down a set of rules.

When I was a fairly new parent, I learned a technique that has been immensely helpful through the years, even now with my adult children when they lived with us. Write down the expectations (and in the case of parenting small children, the consequences). Make it clear: This is how we behave. You can protest all you want, but there is no ambiguity. This is the rule. We don't treat each other poorly anymore. It takes the emotion out of it.

Insist on the rules.

The worst thing you can do is to adopt a set of rules and not insist that everyone follow them. That creates a set of written rules and another set of unwritten rules. Everyone is now trying to figure out the unwritten rules. The unwritten rules will be followed. I cannot emphasize this enough. You must do this. No exceptions. If someone violated Alan Mulally's expected behaviors during a meeting, he would calmly follow them to their office after the meeting and tell them that we aren't treating people like that anymore. He would say it in love, give them plenty of opportunity to correct their ways, or eventually give them an opportunity to find employment elsewhere. He called it "joyful accountability."

Allow everyone to interact with anyone.

One of your working principles could (and in many domains should) be that anyone should be allowed to directly interact with anyone. How can teams work together if there are unwritten rules that dictate how they interact with one another? A team member should be able to contact a director in another department if they need something. I understand there is context here. There are some domains with security or other legitimate concerns that play into this. But for most organizations, this should be the case. You can even add that the interaction should be fast, relevant, and practical.

If interactions are being done improperly, that's a training issue, not an issue with the fact that the interaction is taking place.

As a leader, you will need to model these interactions in three ways: one, reach out to people at levels lower than yourself as a way of saying that we *should* be talking, even at different levels; two, don't reprimand someone for reaching out to you; three, hold your managers and leaders accountable for reacting poorly when someone reaches out to them.

Free-flowing information and collaboration between teams and levels is that important.

48

CONSTRAINT #4:
BLOATED DECISION-MAKING

I WATCHED FROM the sideline as the basketball was passed from the point guard to the wing, to the baseline, and back to the wing, who was now rapidly "cutting" to the basket, resulting in a quick shot and a made basket. The defense could not adjust to the rapid passes fast enough. The sequence happened too quickly.

The next time down the court, a similar sequence played out. This time, the ball was passed from the point guard to the other wing, who passed the ball to the forward in the middle of the court, who passed the ball down to the center, who had snuck behind the defense down by the hoop. Another shot, another basket.

To the casual observer, it may appear to be a finely sequenced play in which the girls knew exactly where they were going to pass the ball to next. As the coach, I knew differently. In reality, I had no idea how the play would unfold each time that our point guard brought the ball down the court.

What they were executing was a pass and cut system that gave the players freedom to make "in the moment" choices within the context of a few simple rules. It's not unlike Phil Jackson's NBA triangle offense where players had a number of options to act while staying within the plan. Okay, maybe our offense wasn't quite at the level of Phil Jackson, but you get the point.

The beauty of this type of thinking on the basketball court is that the players can operate quickly, instantly reacting to the defense, without having to follow the regimented steps of a play that has no flexibility and without waiting for the coach to tell them what to do from the sideline.

The beauty of this type of thinking in your organization is that your teams can operate quickly, instantly reacting to changing conditions, without having to follow regimented steps of a decision-making process that has no flexibility, and without waiting for leaders to tell them what to do from the sideline.

My guess is that if I was sitting across from you, you would be peppering me with story after story about bloated, even detrimental, decision-making processes. Here are a couple of stories that I was told just in the weeks before writing this section.

There's a certain family relation of mine who works in software development who needed to create a new database table on a production server for a client. If you know anything about databases, that is a pretty simple request. Do changes need to be controlled? Absolutely. But this is a fairly minor change. What he got back was a form to complete that took three hours to fill out. You and I both know how long a decision will actually take once that form is completed.

What's interesting is that both parties have a legitimate interest. They both have agendas that are being judged: One party is being judged on reliable, secure production systems, the other party on producing software that makes and saves money. The point is that the decision process is a constraint that prevents them from working together at a high level.

At lunch the other day, I was describing the premise of this book to another family relation who works in sales. He threw up his hands and quickly recounted how he "throws things over the wall [of his department] and has no idea what he's going to get back." The decision-making process was too complicated. "I don't have time to fill out these 37 questions—I'm here to bring in money for the company," he stated in frustration.

I could go on. With the advent of technology and the desire to reach consensus, decision-making becomes so broad and cumbersome as to destroy everything you've worked toward to get teams working together. It must be fixed.

How do we remove decision-making as a constraint and turn it into an advantage so that the people on the point of the spear—the people on the front lines—can work together and make the right decisions quickly? Follow this four-step process for better decision-making.

Step 1: Trust the people on the front lines

This isn't quite as easy as it sounds. In fact, it sounds a bit cliche-ish. And you know what? It is cliche-ish, not because it's not true but because we don't know how to actually trust people on the front lines.

We first have to recognize that we need to end up here: trusting the people on the front lines to make decisions. They have their "feet on the ground." It's like Tom Selleck's character in an episode of the TV series *Blue Bloods* when, as police commissioner, he was watching a scene unfold via video feed and stated to his commanders that "We trust the officer on the scene."

The problem is we don't feel we can just turn people loose and let them decide whatever they want to decide. And you would be right. That's why you first have to...

Step 2: Adopt the law of the blend

Should leaders give their managers and front line team members freedom to make decisions on their own, or should they exhibit control over their employees' decisions?

The answer is yes. It is a blend of both.

Employees without the freedom to make decisions in the moment will operate more slowly and won't be able to work well together. If they have any level of ambition and passion, they will get frustrated by the lack of power they have in order to do what they know is in the best interest of the customer and the company. They'll quit and leave. Or worse, they'll quit and stay.

On the flip side, giving employees complete freedom to make decisions can be counter-productive—especially if those employees do not have a holistic big picture and their decisions are not congruent with what's most important.

The answer is a blend: Give employees simple guidelines in which to operate (rules), continued conversation to understand the guidelines, and the collective awareness to know what everyone is doing.

It's like my basketball team. They have specific guidelines and complete freedom within the context of those guidelines.

In your case, the guidelines or "rules" come from:

1. The three organizational bearings, and
2. The constant collective awareness.

When team members are clear, it's much easier to trust them to make the right decisions.

I'll give you a quick example. Southwest Airlines has been successful for many reasons, not the least of which is clear direction. Specifically, they have three anchors that define how they will be successful and what sets them apart: (1) being on-time, (2) low fares, and (3) loyal customers. Knowing these three anchors is one of Patrick Lencioni's six key questions, which are covered in Part 1: Simplify the Destination. Every employee knows this. And their people are empowered to go and do things that help build those three anchors. This is freedom within the context of specific "guidelines."

Naturally, this depends on the nature of the decision. As James Clear, author of *Atomic Habits* says, "If a decision is reversible, the biggest risk is moving too slow. If a decision is irreversible, the biggest risk is moving too fast." This is good advice to guide the level of decision-making freedom.

If you're uneasy, look at this as a progression. Give your employees more decision-making responsibility, and for being good stewards with those responsibilities, reward them with more decision-making responsibilities. It doesn't have to be an all-or-nothing proposition.

Step 3: Get out of the way, but stay connected

McKinsey, a top consulting company, advocates that after you provide clarity, get out of the way, but stay connected. Staying connected gives you confidence that leaders and managers are making the right decisions. Staying connected gives them a feedback mechanism so they build the confidence that they are making correct decisions. Staying connected provides them with more information as to your intent.

You never turn them loose and just hope for the best. There's always an ongoing conversation.

Step 4: Look for ways to streamline decision processes

As you uncover areas where decision-making is onerous, streamline them. Perhaps task someone or a group of people with streamlining decision processes. Better yet, for straightforward decision processes, just fix them.

By improving how decisions are made, you make it easier for teams to work together across the organization.

49

CONSTRAINT #5:
ILL-EQUIPPED LEADERS

WHILE LEADERSHIP DEVELOPMENT is a topic of great importance and one I enjoy, read about, and conduct workshops about, this is not a book on how to develop leaders. It's a book about how to get teams, departments, and divisions to work together. There are plenty of excellent books on the topic of leadership from the likes of John Maxwell, Stephen Covey, Ken Blanchard, Simon Sinek, and many others.

And yet, how leaders lead across the organization can make or break the formula and cannot simply be ignored.

In these times of change, uncertainty, and new generations in the workforce, we need a breed of "new leaders." We need leaders who don't believe that they have to be in total control at all times but who understand that it's courageous to be vulnerable, leaders who don't always have to be right but who understand that their team members know more than they do, leaders who don't need to get credit but who are satisfied with the success of their team and their customers, leaders who don't lose sleep over their own success but lose sleep over the success of the people on their team, leaders who recognize that it's no longer about them but about empowering others.

Dr. Paul Sternberg, the Chief Medical Officer of Vanderbilt University Medical Center, talks about the transition to a leadership role. "You spend so much of your professional drive focusing on your own level of success to set you up for the next level, but the skills that make you a good *candidate* for the next job have very little to do with your *success* at that next job," he says. You have to change the focus from your own success to the success of the team.

Part of this focus is leadership by influence: the necessity of creating the trust and the ability to get things done, even when you can't tell people what to do. Leaders today are being asked to collaboratively pull together people from multiple departments to create a practice that works well.

Just like the key to healthy leaders and high-functioning teams is setting the context around them, so it is here. The problem is not so much the individual leaders and managers. It's too easy to say that this person or that person is a bad manager. The problem is more that we promote the wrong people, not recognizing that leadership skills are different than technical skills, and we don't provide adequate training and support resources when we do promote people.

As you look at changing the context around teams, don't forget to look at your leaders and managers. Invest time and energy into proactively developing and mentoring them and not throwing them into leadership roles without the resources to succeed. It has a direct effect on the ability of individual teams to thrive and for multiple teams to work together.

SUMMARY OF KEY POINTS

If the organizational systems around teams are not operating properly around them, your teams won't work together.

There are five common organizational constraints that have a negative effect on teams working together:

1. Energy vampires
2. Ineffective rewards
3. Poor treatment of others
4. Ineffective decision-making
5. Ill-equipped leaders

Visit TheHippoSolution.com/bookresources for assessments, downloads, and additional resources.

IMMEDIATE ACTION STEPS

Take one of these quick action steps to take immediate action:

- Visit the book resource page to assess this variable for your organization.
- Create your own Chart of Expected Behaviors.
  Create your own list of behaviors—how we treat each other—and share it with everyone and in every meeting. Hold your leaders accountable for following it.
- Reach out to levels below you.
  Model communication across the organization by communicating with levels that are lower than your current level.
- Model simpler decision-making.
  Select one decision and take yourself out of the decision-making process every Thursday (or pick a "take myself out of a decision" day).
- Read The Energy Bus by Jon Gordon.
  Learn about getting rid of "energy vampires" and having the right kind of energy on your bus.
- Support your leadership development program.
  Go talk to your HR leader(s) about a leadership development program, including mentoring around developing teamwork.

CONCLUDING THOUGHTS: WHERE TO GO FROM HERE

As I sat on the taxiway at the Air Force base, I wondered what would happen next, realizing that I had landed at the wrong airport—the wrong destination. Would I be arrested? Would my mother ever hear from me again?

An air traffic controller's voice sternly began talking to me over the radio. He had been trying to reach me the entire approach. Finding yourself where you didn't expect to be causes you to finally see and hear what you wouldn't see and hear before. I had ignored all of the visual and aural inputs because they didn't match what I "knew" to be true about the situation.

"8323 niner"—that was my call sign—"stay where you are and follow the guide truck to the ramp." "Roger that," I said in as confident a voice as I could muster. In reality, my palms were sweaty, and I was scared. I had no idea how this would unfold.

In a minute, out came a Jeep with a literal "follow me" sign on the back. I followed the Jeep. It seemed to take forever as we taxied across the airport to the ramp. Part of me wanted to get there and get this over with. The other part of me just wanted to turn around, take off, and pretend this never happened.

I was directed to a parking spot. I parked, then went through my checklist to shut down the engine and the rest of the airplane systems.

Out came the military police.

They lifted their rifles and surprisingly pointed them at another small airplane on the ramp. It was standard operating procedure for the military police to come out with their rifles, but they had mistakenly picked the wrong airplane. Those rifles should have been pointed at me.

I got out of the airplane.

What would be the price for landing at the wrong destination—for landing at an Air Force base?

What will be the price when you don't reach your destination? For some, it is the company's survival. For others, it is your job or promotion. For many, it is the extra time and energy that shouldn't be needed to deal with the distractions of going slower and not working together. For most, it is that feeling, the lack of accomplishment, the frustration of not working together, the knowing it shouldn't be this way, the gnawing feeling that we should have accomplished more, the wondering why this is so difficult. Why can't we just be one team?

After a few moments of awkwardly standing on the ramp at the Air Force base, as the military police had their sights on the wrong pilot, an officer strode across the ramp to me.

I expected a boot-camp style gruffness.

Instead, the officer was polite and started a conversation.

He asked me several questions.

He offered to let me talk to the controllers.

It turns out that I was not the first one to accidentally land on their base. The base's runway is almost exactly the same direction as the airport at which I had intended to land. The base is located over a strait of water, just like my target airport. The base was just a few miles south of my intended destination, and so, it was easy to get confused. Well, except for the fact that the base is much bigger, the runways much longer, and the big hangar with "Patrick Air Force Base" painted on it.

I expected handcuffs. The officer gave me grace. The officer told me that the Air Force would not "turn me in." He let me go on my way. I guess I didn't look like I was much of a threat—and fortunately, this was pre-9/11.

I received another chance.

I would learn from this experience and always, always be sure that I reached the correct destination in the future.

For all of us, there is another chance—another opportunity to unleash our teams.

If you do the same things that you are doing now, the future will look like today. You'll reach the same destinations in the same way, if you reach them at all. But if you take different steps, different actions, if you look at organizational teamwork multi-dimensionally, you will get to the correct destination faster, easier, and together.

The distance between not working together and working together is not the gulf that we think it to be. It starts with taking one small action step—today.

My challenge to every leader is to create a world of organizational teamwork where every person and every team works together cohesively to both achieve significant objectives and to create an environment that is flourishing for everyone involved.

ABOUT THE AUTHOR

Mark Kenny works with leaders who want to make their leadership teams stronger, healthier, and more cohesive while improving strategic alignment and communications throughout their organization.

For over 30 years, Mark has worked to improve the results of teams in several hundred organizations, originally in IT and operations and later in keynote speaking, consulting, and training. As the founder and president of a successful software company, Mark gained extensive experience working with companies such as Mars, Deloitte, Xerox, Siemens, the State of Tennessee, and the U.S. Army. He understands teamwork issues from both the leader and front-line perspective as well as the nuances of working with a variety of industries, including manufacturing, healthcare, technology, government, retail, education, engineering, and financial services.

Mark's passion for teamwork extends beyond the workplace, as a soccer and basketball coach for over 20 years. In addition, Mark is an aviation enthusiast who once obtained his pilot's license, an avid basketball player, and a lifelong Green Bay Packers fan. Mark lives outside of Nashville, Tennessee, with his wife, daughter, and three grown sons.

For more information on Mark's speaking, strategic offsites, consulting, and training services, please contact Mark at:

(615) 854-8070
mark@hipposolutions.com

CONNECT WITH MARK

Mark's passion is developing strong teams. He would love to hear from you if you want to email him at mark@hipposolutions.com. Here's his number if you want to give him a call: (615) 854-8070. You can also connect with him on LinkedIn.

Mark is available to work with you on developing a stronger leadership team through offsites, coaching, and consulting. He also loves the opportunity to engage your team, organization, or audience through speaking. If you are interested in having Mark come to your event, visit his website at HippoSolutions.com.

REVIEW INQUIRY

Hey, it's Mark here.

I hope you've enjoyed the book, finding it both useful and fun. I have a favor to ask you.

Would you consider giving it a rating wherever you bought the book? Online book stores are more likely to promote a book when they feel good about its content, and reader reviews are a great barometer for a book's quality.

So please go to the website of wherever you bought the book, search for my name and the book title, and leave a review. If able, perhaps consider adding a picture of you holding the book. That increases the likelihood your review will be accepted!

Many thanks in advance,

Mark Kenny

WILL YOU SHARE THE LOVE?

Get this book for a friend, associate, or family member!

If you have found this book valuable and know others who would find it useful, consider buying them a copy as a gift. Special bulk discounts are available if you would like your whole team or organization to benefit from reading this. Just contact Hippo Solutions at info@hipposolutions.com, or visit our website at HippoSolutions.com for current contact information.